DOS
FOR
DUMMIES®

Quick
Reference
3rd Edition

by Greg Harvey

Hungry Minds™
HUNGRY MINDS, INC.

New York, NY ◆ Cleveland, OH ◆ Indianapolis, IN

DOS For Dummies® Quick Reference, 3rd Edition

Published by
Hungry Minds, Inc.
909 Third Avenue
New York, NY 10022
www.hungryminds.com
www.dummies.com

Library of Congress Catalog Card No.: 98-84652

ISBN: 0-7645-0368-5

Printed in the United States of America

10 9 8 7 6

3O/QU/QV/QR/IN

Distributed in the United States by Hungry Minds, Inc.

Distributed by CDG Books Canada Inc. for Canada; by Transworld Publishers Limited in the United Kingdom; by IDG Norge Books for Norway; by IDG Sweden Books for Sweden; by IDG Books Australia Publishing Corporation Pty. Ltd. for Australia and New Zealand; by TransQuest Publishers Pte Ltd. for Singapore, Malaysia, Thailand, Indonesia, and Hong Kong; by Gotop Information Inc. for Taiwan; by ICG Muse, Inc. for Japan; by Intersoft for South Africa; by Eyrolles for France; by International Thomson Publishing for Germany, Austria and Switzerland; by Distribuidora Cuspide for Argentina; by LR International for Brazil; by Galileo Libros for Chile; by Ediciones ZETA S.C.R. Ltda. for Peru; by WS Computer Publishing Corporation, Inc., for the Philippines; by Contemporanea de Ediciones for Venezuela; by Express Computer Distributors for the Caribbean and West Indies; by Micronesia Media Distributor, Inc. for Micronesia; by Chips Computadoras S.A. de C.V. for Mexico; by Editorial Norma de Panama S.A. for Panama; by American Bookshops for Finland.

For general information on Hungry Minds' products and services please contact our Customer Care Department within the U.S. at 800-762-2974, outside the U.S. at 317-572-3993 or fax 317-572-4002.

For sales inquiries and reseller information, including discounts, premium and bulk quantity sales, and foreign-language translations, please contact our Customer Care Department at 800-434-3422, fax 317-572-4002, or write to Hungry Minds, Inc., Attn: Customer Care Department, 10475 Crosspoint Boulevard, Indianapolis, IN 46256.

For information on licensing foreign or domestic rights, please contact our Sub-Rights Customer Care Department at 650-653-7098.

For information on using Hungry Minds' products and services in the classroom or for ordering examination copies, please contact our Educational Sales Department at 800-434-2086 or fax 317-572-4005.

For press review copies, author interviews, or other publicity information, please contact our Public Relations department at 317-572-3168 or fax 317-572-4168.

For authorization to photocopy items for corporate, personal, or educational use, please contact Copyright Clearance Center, 222 Rosewood Drive, Danvers, MA 01923, or fax 978-750-4470.

Hungry Minds™ is a trademark of Hungry Minds, Inc.

About the Author

Greg Harvey, the author of over 50 computer books, has had a long career of teaching business people in the use of IBM PC, Windows, and Macintosh software application programs. From 1983 to 1988, he conducted hands-on computer software training for corporate business users with a variety of training companies (including his own, PC Teach). From 1988 to 1992, he taught university classes in Lotus 1-2-3 and Introduction to Database Management Technology (using dBASE) in the Department of Information Systems at Golden Gate University in San Francisco.

In mid-1993, Greg started a new multimedia publishing venture, mind over media, Inc. As a multimedia developer and computer book author, he hopes to enliven his future online computer books by making them into true interactive learning experiences that will vastly enrich and improve the training of users of all skill levels.

Visit his Web site at www.mindovermedia.com and send him your feedback on this book at gharvey@mindovermedia.com.

Acknowledgments

I am indebted to a number of people on this project. I want to thank all of the following people who worked so hard in various and sundry (and sometimes, even mysterious) ways to make this 3rd edition of the book a reality:

Ellen Camm and Mary Bednarek for getting the ball rolling.

Jamie Marcum for his contribution of DOS-under-Windows-98 material for this edition.

Jim McCarter for his contributions to the second and third editions.

Susan Christophersen for shepherding this edition through all of its editiorial phases.

Kevin McCarter for the tech review and the amazing and FAST layout folks in Production.

Last, but never least, I want to acknowledge my indebtedness to Dan Gookin, whose vision, sardonic wit, and (sometimes) good humor produced *DOS For Dummies,* the "Mother" of all *...For Dummies* books. Thanks for the inspiration and the book that made it all possible, Dan.

Greg Harvey
Point Reyes Station, California

Publisher's Acknowledgments

We're proud of this book; please send us your comments through our Online Registration Form located at: www.dummies.com.

Some of the people who helped bring this book to market include the following:

Acquisitions, Development, and Editorial

Project Editor: Susan Christophersen

Acquisitions Editor: Ellen Camm

Permissions Editor: Heather Dismore

Technical Editor: Kevin McCarter

Editorial Manager: Mary C. Corder

Editorial Assistant: Michael D. Sullivan

Production

Project Coordinator: Karen York

Layout and Graphics: Traci Ankrom, Lou Boudreau, Linda M. Boyer, Maridee V. Ennis, Angela F. Hunckler, Jane E. Martin, Brent Savage, M. Anne Sipahimalani, Deirdre Smith, Michael A. Sullivan

Proofreaders: Christine Berman, Kelli Botta, Rebecca Senninger, Janet M. Withers

Indexer: Sherry Massey

General and Administrative

Hungry Minds, Inc.: John Kilcullen, CEO; Bill Barry, President and COO; John Ball, Executive VP, Operations & Administration; John Harris, CFO

Hungry Minds Technology Publishing Group: Richard Swadley, Senior Vice President and Publisher; Mary Bednarek, Vice President and Publisher, Networking and Certification; Walter R. Bruce III, Vice President and Publisher, General User and Design Professional; Joseph Wikert, Vice President and Publisher, Programming; Mary C. Corder, Editorial Director, Branded Technology Editorial; Andy Cummings, Publishing Director, General User and Design Professional; Barry Pruett, Publishing Director, Visual

Hungry Minds Manufacturing: Ivor Parker, Vice President, Manufacturing

Hungry Minds Marketing: John Helmus, Assistant Vice President, Director of Marketing

Hungry Minds Production for Branded Press: Debbie Stailey, Production Director

Hungry Minds Sales: Roland Elgey, Senior Vice President, Sales and Marketing; Michael Violano, Vice President, International Sales and Sub Rights

◆

The publisher would like to give special thanks to Patrick J. McGovern, without whom this book would not have been possible.

◆

Contents at a Glance

Table of Contents

How to Use This Book

You've all heard of online help. Well, just think of this book as onside help. Keep it by your side when you're at the computer, and *before* you try to use a DOS command that you're the least bit unsure of (like all 88, or however many there are now), look up the command in the appropriate section. Scan the entry, looking for any warnings (those bomb icons). Follow the "DOSspeak" section to compose the command at the DOS prompt, then check it over carefully, knock on wood or cross yourself (whatever's right), and press the Enter key.

This Intro gives you more details on how to know what you're supposed to type and how to use the little pictures *(icons)* scattered throughout the book.

DOS: An Operating System Only Someone Else's Mother Could Love

Welcome to *DOS For Dummies Quick Reference,* 3rd Edition, a quick reference that looks at the lighter side of DOS commands (such as it is). I mean, who could take seriously a command such as

```
DEFRAG [drive:] [/f] [/s[:]order] [/b] [/skiphigh]
    [lcd | /bw | /g0] [/h]
```

a DOS 7.1 command for optimizing disk performance? *Defrag* and *skiphigh* sound like words right out of a Pentagon code book. And look at all those /f and /s doodads. About the only thing that seems halfway intelligible here is the /g0 business, as in "let's get outta here." But even *that's* not "go" (gee-oh), but "g0" (gee-zero). So go figure. To paraphrase the great comic, "Take my DOS, *please!*"

Ah, if only DOS were really just a laughing matter! Much as we may poke fun at the DOS vocabulary, grammar, and syntax (DOS is such an easy target, kinda like a politician), we've all heard tell of the disastrous results of misusing common commands such as FORMAT or ERASE. And these major and minor catastrophes with DOS often come about as the result of little errors, perhaps as small as a misplaced star (*) or space in the command, a typo in the filename, or a semicolon where a colon ought to be.

As a means of staving off such disasters at the DOS prompt, I offer you *DOS For Dummies Quick Reference,* 3rd Edition. This book gives you the lowdown on each and every DOS command (except FDISK, a command I guarantee you'll never miss), alerting you to oddities and potential pitfalls (see "The Cast of Icons" later in this Intro).

For convenience, this book is divided into five sections. The first section introduces you to DOS. The second section details the newest version of DOS, running under Windows 98. The third section contains all the DOS commands, listed in alphabetical order from APPEND to XCOPY. The fourth section contains all the batch commands, listed in alphabetical order from @ to SHIFT. The fifth section contains a list of the configuration commands in alphabetical order from BREAK to SWITCHES. And there's also a glossary at the end, "Techie Talk," in case you stumble over some of the terms that you come across in this book.

Regardless of what section you find it in, each command is handled in a similar way. Below the command name, you find a brief description of its function. Below the description is the

"DOSspeak" section (which the other quick references insist on calling the *syntax*). Here, you are exposed to all the gobbledygook that it takes to make this command go (please see "Parlez-Vous DOSspeak?" later in this Intro for decoding instructions). First, you encounter the command line and then — after you recover from that shock — you see a table explaining exactly what all that junk in the command line means.

Following the "DOSspeak" section, in most cases, you'll find a "Sample" section that gives you some examples of how you might use this command in real life. A cast of characters, which includes folks such as Cousin Olaf and the Boss, pop in and out of the command examples found in the "Sample" section.

Parlez-Vous DOSspeak?

Remember those Little Orphan Annie decoding rings? As I understand it, those rings had little devices on the top that you could use to decode Annie's "secret" message for the week. The announcer read the secret messages at the end of the radio programs — real bogus things such as "Consume vast quantities of Ovaltine" that the enemy was supposedly keen to intercept. To decode one of these gems, you wrote down the coded letters; then, at your leisure, you used the ring to turn each coded letter into English!

Don't you wish they made a Little Orphan Annie DOSspeak decoding ring so that when you came upon a line of DOSspeak such as

```
FORMAT drive:[/v[:label] [/q] [/u] [/f:size] [/b]
       [/s]
```

all you had to do was dial up each of the coded parts on your ring to find out what they meant in English? (Wouldn't you be surprised to find out that the secret message here is "Consume vast quantities of Microsoft products"?)

Short of this mythical DOSspeak decoding ring, I have endeavored to give you all the keys you need to decode typical DOSspeak lines such as the preceding FORMAT example. Just match the word or funny-looking / thing, called a *switch,* in the DOSspeak line with the word or / thing in the table that describes each option. Doing that kind of "word-for-word" translation will give you a basic idea of what it is you're telling DOS to do when you use these things.

Along with this word-for-word translation, you need to have a rudimentary understanding of DOSspeak grammar. That's where the different typographic conventions used in the DOSspeak line come into play.

✦ The things you *must* include in the DOS command to get it to do anything are printed in **bold** type. If you look back at the earlier FORMAT example, you'll see that of all the many things that appear in this line, only FORMAT and *drive:* are required.

✦ Optional things in the command line are enclosed in brackets, which, by the way, you don't actually include when typing the stuff inside them at the DOS prompt.

In addition to the distinction between required (bold) and optional (nonbold enclosed in brackets) stuff, you will also find a distinction between stuff you type verbatim and stuff that you substitute with your own information.

✦ Stuff you type verbatim is shown in regular type.

✦ Stuff you replace with some other information — otherwise known as *variables* — is shown in *italics*.

Harkening back to the FORMAT example, of the two pieces of information that you have to give, FORMAT and *drive:*, you enter FORMAT verbatim (although you don't have to capitalize the letters — this is just a typographic convention). In place of the word *drive:*, you enter the letter of the drive with the disk you want to format, such as a: or b:.

Some DOS commands make you choose between alternative values. Choices between one thing and another in DOSspeak are shown by a | (vertical bar known as a pipe character, although it looks a lot more like a pipe cleaner) between the alternatives. For example, if you look up the VERIFY command in this book, you'll see the DOSspeak line

```
VERIFY [on | off]
```

Now, keeping in mind our DOSspeak grammar rules, only the command name VERIFY is absolutely essential because it's in bold, whereas the [on | off] part is enclosed in brackets.

If you enter VERIFY all by itself, DOS tells you the current status of disk verification — that is, whether it's on or off. If, however, you want to change the status of disk verification, you must then add the on or off optional parameter to the command. You know that you must choose one or the other and not try to enter both because there's a pipe | thingy between them. You also know that after you've chosen one, you must enter it verbatim because neither one is in italics. Therefore, to turn on disk verification, you enter

```
verify on
```

at the DOS prompt. To turn it off, you enter

```
verify off
```

That's about all there is to decoding either the Dead Sea Scrolls or DOSspeak command lines. With just a little bit of practice, you can be decoding your secret DOSspeak messages faster than Annie could say, "Drink your Ovaltine."

The Cast of Icons

In your travels with the DOS commands in this book, you'll come across the following icons:

Pay attention! This tip could save you some time.

Look out! There's some little something in this command that can get you into trouble.

Here's where things get weird. DOS has more than its share of quirks, and this icon marks some of them.

This command bit the dust in DOS 6 — Rest In Peace.

This icon points you to the appropriate section of *DOS For Dummies,* Windows 98 Edition (by Dan Gookin; IDG Books Worldwide, Inc.), for more information about running DOS under Windows 98.

Part 1

Getting to Know DOS

The first half of this part gives you the absolute basics — on files, directories, disk drives, that kind of stuff. If you're familiar with computers, go ahead and skip to the second half of this part, which tells you how to enter commands, get help, and use wildcards. If you need more information on DOS than that, see Dan Gookin's *DOS For Dummies,* 3rd Edition (IDG Books Worldwide, Inc.).

In this part . . .

- ✔ **Organizing information in files and directories**

- ✔ **Telling DOS what to do: using commands**

- ✔ **Using wildcard characters to indicate groups of files**

- ✔ **Finding out which version of DOS you're running**

- ✔ **Getting help with DOS commands**

Basic Elements

DOS is an acronym that stands for *D*isk *O*perating *S*ystem. This operating system has been around for a long time, ever since the first IBM Personal Computer was introduced. That early version of DOS wasn't very user friendly. Come to think of it, neither is the current version. The good news is that no matter which version of DOS you encounter, it functions in essentially the same way as all the others. Oh sure, each new version has added new features, but the basics are the same.

What do you do with this DOS thing? You use it to tell your computer what to do. Hey! You get to be in charge! All you need to do is figure out how to talk to DOS. You talk to DOS by typing commands on the keyboard. The DOS command line interpreter tries to make sense of what you type, and, if successful, it passes the command along to the computer in a format that the hardware can understand.

But before you fuddle your mind with that stuff, you should have a good grasp of the basics: files, directories, and disk drives.

Files and directories

A *file* is a collection of information stored on a disk. Files fall into three main categories: programs, data, and directories. Yes, I could give you a million subcategories, but these three will suffice for now. *Program files* contain instructions that tell the computer what to do. *Data files* are the information created when you use program files. An example of a program file is WINWORD.EXE, the Microsoft Word word processing program that I used for typing this part. An example of a data file is how this part that you're reading right now is stored on my computer.

A *directory* is a special type of file for organizing program and data files on disk. A directory can contain program files, data files, and other directories.

In order to tell one file from another, you assign names to the files. Filenames must adhere to certain rules. In DOS, the filename itself can consist of one to eight characters (**see also** Part II for more on filenames under Windows 98). The *extension,* which is usually supplied by the program that created the file and which indicates to your computer how to deal with the file, can be one to three characters. The filename and the extension are separated by a period. Valid characters are letters, numbers, and some special symbols, such as @ # $ % ~ ^ &. Even though these symbols are permitted, I suggest that you stick to letters and numbers to be on the safe side.

You may have heard that directories are now called *folders*. This has been true since Windows 95 arrived on the scene. However, because most DOS commands and utilities still refer to directories, I use the term *directories* throughout this book. If you run into any wild-eyed Windows 98 fanatics, just remember to say folder when you mean directory. No sense in provoking them unneccesarily.

When naming a file, remember to make the name reflect the contents of the file so that you won't have to open and close a dozen files before you find the one you're looking for.

Here's an example of a *legal* (meaning that DOS will allow you to use it and won't send you nasty error messages) filename:

```
letter1.doc
```

Note: DOS filenames are not case sensitive, so LETTER1.DOC, letter1.doc, and Letter1.doc are the same, as far as DOS is concerned.

Disk drives and disks

Disk drives are the physical devices that you use to store files. There are many different types of disk drives, such as hard disk drives, floppy disk drives, and CD-ROM drives. All disks store information in files, and all files are stored in directories. Disk drives differ mainly in speed and capacity. Floppy disk drives and CD-ROM drives use removable disks, whereas the hard disk drive (except on the newest laptops) always remains inside your computer.

Just as files must have names, disk drives must have names. A disk drive name consists of a letter of the alphabet between A and Z. You usually need to follow the letter with a colon when you're referring to it in a command to DOS. The first floppy disk drive in your computer is always named A. The second floppy disk drive in your computer is always named B. The first hard disk drive in your computer is always named C, even if your computer doesn't have a second floppy disk drive. If you have a CD-ROM drive in or attached to your computer, it may be named D. If you're on a network, the network drives may be anywhere from D (or E, if you do have a CD-ROM drive) to Z.

You need to prepare a disk to hold files, a process called *formatting* (you use the FORMAT command — *see* Part III). Formatting a disk erases any files and directories that may be on it and creates a directory known as the *root directory*. The root directory is represented by the \ character. You can use DOS commands to create additional directories in the root directory.

A typical hard disk drive contains directories for *applications* (which are productivity programs, such as Excel or WordPerfect), data, and games. These directories can contain files and other directories.

Pathnames

A pathname is a file's address, showing the hierarchy of directories and drives that DOS needs to go through to get to the file. A complete pathname includes the drive, the directory or directories, and the filename. If you specify a filename only, DOS expects to find the file in the current directory. The pathname

```
C:\DATA\LETTERS\LETTER3.DOC
```

indicates a file named LETTER3.DOC located in the LETTERS subdirectory (a directory within a directory is referred to as a *subdirectory*), which is located in the DATA directory, which in turn is located in the root \ of drive C.

Pathnames, which you read left to right, go from the general to the specific. Directory names and filenames are separated by the \ character.

Entering Commands

Before you begin entering DOS commands, you should understand the command prompt. In DOS, the command prompt is often called the *DOS prompt.* The DOS prompt is your cue that the computer is waiting for you to type a command.

The DOS prompt often consists of the current drive and directory followed by >, as in this example:

```
C:\PROGRAMS>_
```

Immediately following the DOS prompt is a blinking underscore, which is where the letter you type will appear.

DOS allows you to customize the DOS prompt — *see* PROMPT in Part III.

Entering a DOS command is simply (ha!) a matter of typing the command followed by any parameters and switches. A *parameter* is the object that the command will act on. The parameter is often a filename. A *switch* modifies the way in which the command is performed. Switches are preceded by the / character. Some commands do not require any parameters or switches. Look up the command in the appropriate part of this book to find out more.

After you type the command, press Enter. This is the signal to DOS that you are finished typing the command and any parameters and switches. If you do not press Enter, the computer will wait and wait and wait and . . . .

Spelling counts! (And you thought computers were smart.) Computers are very obedient devices. They make every attempt to do *exactly* what you tell them. DOS assumes that you know what you're doing; it does what you type rather than what you mean. (After all, how could it possibly know what you mean?)

Case does not count. Just as in filenames, DOS couldn't care less whether you type everything in all CAPITAL LETTERS, all lower-case letters, or a CoMbInAtIoN oF tHe TwO.

When you're finished typing a DOS command at the prompt, don't forget to press the Enter key. Be careful not to press Enter in the middle of a command — you won't get the expected results.

Help with DOS Commands

HELP!! HELP!! Yelling help doesn't do much for you, does it? How do you get help with that DOS command? This book is a good resource. Look up the command in here or check the DOS manual (last resort) that came with your computer system.

You also have a couple of ways to get help on-screen, if you're running DOS Version 5.0 or later. If you need to know the command syntax (DOSspeak — the way the command should be typed and what parameters and switches are available) and don't have this book handy, type the command name followed by a space and /?, like this:

```
COPY /?
```

Typing this command results in something like the following:

```
Copies one or more files to another location.

COPY [/A | /B] source [/A | /B] [+ source [/A | /B]
     [+ ...]] [destination [/A | /B] [/V] [/Y | /-Y]

source        Specifies the file or files to be copied.
/A            Indicates an ASCII text file.
/B            Indicates a binary file.
destination   Specifies the directory and/or
              filename for the new file(s).
```

And so on.

If you want to see examples of a DOS command, type **HELP** followed by the name of the command. Do not include any parameters or switches. When you type

```
HELP Tree
```

and press Enter, you get a screen like the following.

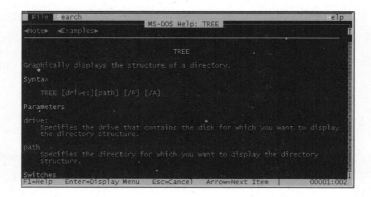

You can use the arrow keys to navigate this screen. To view the Note or Example (at the top of the screen), press Tab or use the arrow keys to place the cursor between the two outward-pointing arrows, and then press Enter. Press Esc to return to the previous screen.

But what if you can't remember the command name that you want to look up? Well, if Al in Finance still hasn't given you back your copy of *DOS For Dummies Quick Reference,* 3rd Edition, type HELP at the DOS prompt. You'll be greeted by a screen that looks like the following figure.

To exit the Help program, press Alt+F, X —(which means that you press the Alt key and the F key simultaneously, release both keys, and then press the X key). *F* and *X* are called *hot keys*. You can usually tell what hot keys to use with the Alt combination by looking at the file or command name and seeing which letter is bold or underlined. When you exit, you press Alt+F to open the File menu and then X to choose the Exit command. (Yeah, that's just as intuitive as anything else you'll come across with computers.)

 If you're using the version of DOS that is included with Windows 98, you won't be able to use the Help program unless you copy the files HELP.EXE and HELP.HLP from the \OTHER\OLDMSDOS directory of the CD-ROM. *See also* Part II for details.

Version Determination

How can you tell which version of DOS you're running — and why should you care? The how is simple. Type VER and press Enter. DOS obediently displays the version of DOS that is currently running. You may see something such as MS-DOS Version 6.22. *MS* indicates that the version of DOS you're using was created by Microsoft. (Other versions of DOS exist, such as IBM-DOS.) You may even see something such as Windows 98. [Version 4.10.1650]. This response indicates that you're running the version of DOS included with Windows 98.

Now that you know what version you have, why should you care? Well, you probably don't, but your software does. When software developers create DOS programs, they may want to take advantage of the features that a certain version of DOS provides. This usually means that the program will not run on an older version of DOS. When you purchase software, look on the box for the System Requirements, where you'll usually find what version of DOS the program requires (if it's a DOS-based program) and what minimum hardware the program requires to run.

Wildcard Characters

Sometimes you want to use a command on a whole group of files, or you're not sure of the exact spelling of a filename. DOS provides you with a couple of special *wildcard characters*. Wildcard characters are similar to the Jokers in a deck of cards: They can stand for any other character.

?	Substitutes for any single character.
*	Substitutes for any number of characters.

?OG would specify all filenames that have three characters, with *O* and *G* as the second and third characters, respectively. HOG, DOG, LOG, and FOG would all match. FROG, SMOG, and GROG would not, because they have *four* characters — the ? character substitutes for only a single character.

*OG would specify all filenames that have at least two characters, with *O* and *G* as the last two characters. OG, HOG, LOG, FOG, FROG, SMOG, GROG, and KELLOG would all match. KELLOGG would not, because the last two characters are *GG*.

Be careful when using wildcard characters — you may go further than you intended and affect files that you didn't want to modify. Don't use wildcard characters when deleting unless you're absolutely positive about what you're doing.

Part II

DOS under Windows 98

Oh where, oh where has my little DOS gone? Oh where, oh where can it be? With its help so short and its commands so long, oh where, oh where can it beeeeee? If you didn't like DOS to begin with, you probably don't catch yourself singing that little ditty too often. Those of you who lament the arrival of the Graphical User Interface (GUI) and pine for the ol' command line interface (yes, both of you) can take heart: DOS has not forsaken you! In fact, DOS has not gone anywhere. It is just hidden in the shadows of that shiny new operating system, Windows 98. I will show you how to politely (that's right, politely; there's no excuse for being rude) ask Windows 98 to step aside so that you may interact with DOS.

In this part . . .

- ✔ Doing DOS with windows
- ✔ Catching up on the old DOS commands: which made the cut and which didn't
- ✔ Getting some old DOS commands off the Windows 98 CD
- ✔ Manipulating those long Windows 98 filenames in DOS
- ✔ Running DOS-based programs and games under Windows 98
- ✔ Rebooting your computer
- ✔ Viruses
- ✔ FAT32

The DOS Prompt

Follow these steps to summon DOS:

1. Click the Start button on the taskbar (the taskbar is that row of pictures for all the currently open programs, as shown in the following figure).

2. Highlight <u>P</u>rograms on the Start menu.

3. Click MS-DOS Prompt on the continuation menu that pops up.

If you're mouse impaired or just very pro-keyboard, you may follow these steps to call DOS:

1. Press Ctrl+Esc.

2. Press P.

3. Press the ↓ key until MS-DOS Prompt is highlighted.

4. Press Enter.

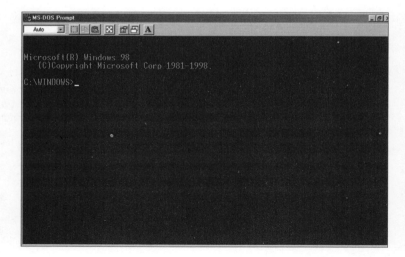

Your efforts are rewarded with the arrival of the DOS window. DOS in a window!? Don't sweat that right now — it comes up later in this section.

When your fingers tire of typing commands, you can put DOS away and return to Windows 98 by typing EXIT and pressing Enter.

If you need to return to Windows 98 but aren't done with DOS just yet, press Alt+Esc. To return to DOS, click the MS-DOS Prompt button on the taskbar (or press Alt+Tab).

You were probably taught to exit all your programs before turning off your computer. This is a good idea. You were also probably taught that it was safe to turn off your computer when you were at the C:\ prompt. This is not such a good idea anymore. To turn off your computer in Windows 98, follow these steps:

1. Exit all open programs, including DOS.

2. Click the Start button and choose Sh<u>u</u>t Down.

3. Make sure that the <u>S</u>hut down radio button is selected and click <u>O</u>K or press Enter.

4. After a few moments, Windows 98 gives you permission to turn off your computer. *That's* when you can flip the off switch.

DOS in a Window

DOS in a window? Yes, alas, DOS no longer runs the show. Having trouble reading the characters in that DOS window? Try maximizing the window: Just click the Maximize button on the title bar — it's the one that looks like a square and is next to the X. Here's what you get now:

Copy — ┌Paste

Mark ┐ ┌Full Screen

Font Size ┌Properties Background Font

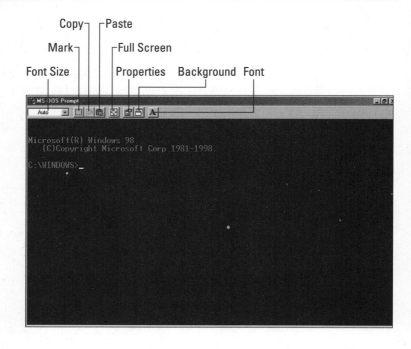

What do you mean, it still doesn't look the same? You find that the title bars, buttons, and menus detract from the DOS atmosphere? Okay, you want DOS to hog the entire screen? Fine. Press Alt+Enter. That's it. Just that one key combination. By the way, Alt+Enter is a toggle — press it again to squeeze DOS back into a window.

Is there a difference between the DOS window and other windows? Yes and no. *Yes* because the DOS window contains the DOS prompt or a DOS-based program. *No* because a window is a window is a window. All windows have certain things in common, such as the title bar and the Minimize, Restore/Maximize, and Close buttons.

Here's what all the buttons are for on the DOS toolbar:

Button or Box	Function
Auto	Font Size drop-down list box. Offers a quickie way of changing the font size, whereas the Font button takes you to a dialog box. You'll usually want to stick to the Auto selection, which makes Windows choose the font size based on the size of the DOS window.
	Mark button, for marking data or text that you want to copy.

Button or Box	Function
	Copy button, for copying text or data to the Windows Clipboard.
	Paste button, for taking a copy of the text or data that's currently on the Clipboard and placing it somewhere else.
	Full Screen button. Puts DOS in full-screen mode. Press Alt+Enter to return to the previous-size MS-DOS Prompt window.
	Properties button. See "Customizing the DOS environment" later in this part.
	Background button. See "Multitasking" in this part.
A	Font button. Takes you to the Font part of the Properties dialog box, which gives you a few options in addition to changing the font size (you can adjust the font size more quickly by simply using the Font Size box on the toolbar).

The best of both worlds

Sometimes you want the computer to do something for you, but you don't want to crank up the appropriate Windows program. For example, you might want to list all the files in a particular directory that have the read-only attribute. For me, typing

```
DIR /AR
```

is much easier than using My Computer or Windows Explorer to display the same information.

I also find renaming groups of files much easier to accomplish from the DOS prompt.

On the other hand, there are some things that I find easier to do from Windows than from the DOS prompt. Copying or moving groups of files with dissimilar names is a snap with Windows Explorer, but a chore from the DOS prompt.

Formatting a disk is a cinch from Windows Explorer, too. Just right-click the floppy drive icon and select Format from the context menu that pops up. Sure beats remembering all those switches and parameters for the FORMAT command.

I like to use Windows to change the system date and time. I just right-click the clock in the taskbar and select Adjust Date / Time. This lets me change the date and time from one dialog box. No more hassles with hh-mm-ss-xx.

Of course, the important thing to remember is to use the method that you are most comfortable with. I tend to use the DOS prompt quite often. But then, I have been using computers since long before Windows and that GUI stuff came along. (Why, when I was a boy, I had to walk five miles in the snow to get to school. . . .)

Extinct DOS Commands

If the DOS commands in the following list are the ones that you held dear, you're going to be disappointed. They are not included in the Windows 98 version of DOS. *Note:* If you upgraded from Windows 3.1, some of these commands may still be lurking around. See "Surviving DOS Commands" later in this part for a list of commands that made the cut.

APPEND	INTERLNK	RECOVER
ASSIGN	INTERSVR	REPLACE
BACKUP	JOIN	RESTORE
COMP	MEMCARD	RAMDRIVE
DOSSHELL	MEMMAKER	ROMDRIVE
EDLIN	MIRROR	SHARE
EGA	MSAV	SMARTMON
FASTHELP	MSBACKUP	TREE
FASTOPEN	POWER	UNDELETE
GRAFTABL	PRINT	UNFORMAT
GRAPHICS	PRINT	VSAFE
HELP	QBASIC	

Actually, SHARE is still around; it made the list because you can't run it from the DOS prompt.

FAT32

What is FAT32 and why should you care? Fat32 is a new version of the File Allocation Table (FAT) file system that lets disks over 2GB be formatted as a single drive. If your hard disk is smaller than 2GB, forget about FAT32. If your hard disk is larger than 2GB, however, you may benefit from converting to FAT32. FAT32 makes more efficient use of disk space, allowing you to store more files (especially if you have lots of small files) and access them more quickly.

To take advantage of the FAT32 benefits, you must run the FAT32 Converter on your hard disk. You run the FAT32 Converter by clicking Start, pointing to Programs, pointing to Accessories, pointing to System Tools, and then clicking FAT32 Converter.

Before you convert to this format, you need to be aware of the following issues:

✦ After you convert your hard drive to the FAT32 format, you cannot return to using the FAT16 format unless you repartition and format the FAT32 drive. Formatting a drive removes *all* files on the drive.

✦ If you have a compressed drive, or think you might want to compress your drive sometime in the future, do not convert to FAT32.

✦ If you have a removable drive that you use with another operating system, don't convert that drive to FAT32.

✦ Hibernate features will not work on a FAT32 drive.

✦ If you convert your hard drive to FAT32, then you cannot uninstall Windows 98. Unless, of course, you repartition and format the drive.

✦ Some disk utilities that depend on the old FAT (now called FAT16) do not work with FAT32 drives. Check with your disk utility manufacturer to see whether it has an updated version that is compatible with FAT32.

✦ If you convert your hard drive to FAT32, you can no longer use dual boot to run earlier versions of Windows (Windows 95 [Version 4.00.950], Windows NT 3.*x,* Windows NT 4.0, and Windows 3.*x*).

Filenames

Microsoft finally bestowed the gift of long filenames upon us. No longer are you tethered to the dreaded 8.3 (eight or fewer characters in the filename, three or fewer characters in the extension) filename specification.

Using those long Windows 98 filenames in DOS

But what happens to those long filenames when you're at the DOS prompt? Nothing. Huh? Well, okay, you do have to work a little harder to see the long filenames, but they are still there. When you're at the DOS prompt, Windows 98 truncates long filenames so that they adhere to the 8.3 specification. Here's an example:

Windows 98 filename: This file has a long filename

Truncated version: THISFI~1

Both of these filenames refer to the same file. The second version is what you get when Windows 98 pares down the long filename to fit the 8.3 specification. Of course, if your Windows 98 filenames are eight characters or fewer, Windows doesn't pare them down at all.

Can you use long filenames at the DOS prompt? Yes, you can. Just enclose the filenames in double quotation marks. Directories are files, so they can have long names, too. Be sure to enclose the entire path in double quotation marks. Of course, you can always use the short version of the filename. Here are a couple of examples:

```
COPY "C:\FILES WITH LONG NAMES\THIS FILE HAS A LONG
    FILENAME" A:\
COPY C:\FILESW~1\THISFI~1 A:\

DEL "THIS FILE HAS A LONG.FILENAME"
DEL THISFI~1
```

Use the method that you are most comfortable with. Personally, I hate to type the ~ thingy.

If you want to see the long filenames from the DOS prompt, just type **DIR** and press Enter. The long filenames are displayed to the right of the file date-time stamp. If you want to see just the long filenames without all the clutter, type **DIR /B** and press Enter. You'll see the files listed in long-name format.

Rebooting Your Computer

Can you press Ctrl+Alt+Delete to reboot your computer? Yes and no. Pressing Ctrl+Alt+Delete causes Windows 98 to display the Close Program dialog box.

Although pressing Ctrl+Alt+Delete while the Close Program dialog box is displayed will reboot your computer, this is *not* a good idea! Windows 98 does not like to be shut down in such an abrupt fashion. There is a collection of files called the Registry that Windows 98 uses to keep track of your computer's hardware and software. Rebooting while these files are open (that is, not politely asking Windows 98 to shut down) could really foul up your configuration. No, it won't blow up your computer, but it may cause you to lose any open documents that you haven't saved, or you may have to reinstall Windows 98 (and who wants to go through that hassle again?).

So, how do you reboot your computer? The recommended procedure is listed in "The DOS Prompt" section of this part. You have to go through the Start menu and choose Shut Down. Only when Windows 98 tells you that it's okay to shut off the computer can you flip that off switch.

So, what is that Close Program dialog box for? It's for times when a program stops responding and pressing keys has no effect. Here's what you do when your program goes zombie on you:

1. Press Ctrl+Alt+Delete to bring up the Close Program dialog box.

2. Click the name of the program that's not responding.

3. Click the End Task button.

If you ever inadvertently press Ctrl+Alt+Delete, click the Cancel button or press Esc to get out of that situation.

Running DOS Programs under Windows 98

Why would you want to run those old DOS programs, such as WordPerfect 5.1 for DOS or 1-2-3 for DOS, under Windows 98? For lots of reasons:

✦ One reason might be that you upgraded to Windows 98 from DOS and had a program such as WordPerfect 5.1 for DOS already installed on your PC. Do you need to upgrade your word processor software to one of those newfangled Windows 98 programs? Well, do you have to buy a new car every time a new model comes out? No. Of course, if you want to take advantage of all the new features that a program such as Word for Windows 98 offers, you will need to upgrade.

✦ Perhaps you don't have money in the budget to upgrade all your old DOS applications at this time. Software can be very expensive (especially when you have a large office with many PCs).

✦ You might have a DOS application that you like (or need) to use that is no longer supported or that is not being offered in a Windows 98 version.

There is a sunny side to running DOS applications under Windows 98: You can run multiple DOS-based and Windows-based applications simultaneously, and switch easily between them. You have a few ways of doing this:

✦ If the application window you want to switch to is visible, simply click anywhere on the window.

✦ Hold down the Alt key and press Tab until the icon representing the program you want to switch to is surrounded by a box. The following figure shows the Word icon in such a box (it's the picture with the *W* on it).

✦ On the taskbar, click the button representing the program you want to switch to.

If the taskbar is not visible, press Ctrl+Esc.

Copying text or graphics from DOS to Windows

You can copy text or graphics from a DOS-based program. Your program needs to be in a window for this to work. If it isn't, just press Alt+Enter to stuff it into a window.

 1. Click the Mark button (the one that looks like a dotted-line box on the toolbar).

2. Click and drag to select your text or graphic.

 3. Click the Copy button — the one that looks like two pieces of paper.

If the Mark button is not visible in the DOS window, do this:

1. Press Alt+Spacebar.

2. Press T (for Toolbar).

The text or graphic that you selected is copied to the Windows 98 Clipboard and is ready to be pasted into another window.

You can paste text from a DOS-based or Windows-based application into a DOS window very easily:

1. Switch to the window into which you would like to paste the text.

2. Click the Paste button (the one that looks like a clipboard).

 If the Paste button is not visible in the DOS window, do this:

1. Press Alt+Spacebar.

2. Press T (for Toolbar).

The text appears in the DOS window just as if you had typed it yourself.

Multitasking

You can *multitask* a DOS program. That is, your DOS program can continue to perform a task (such as sorting a large database) while you switch to another program (such as WordPerfect 5.1 for DOS) and work on something else.

 Multitasking is as easy as this: Click the Background button.

If the Background button is not visible in the DOS window, do this:

> *1.* Press Alt+Spacebar.
>
> *2.* Press T (for <u>T</u>oolbar).

Your DOS program continues to run in the background when you switch to another program.

 For more details on multitasking, ***see also*** *DOS For Dummies,* 3rd Edition, Chapter 6.

Running DOS games under Windows 98

Windows 98 does a great job of running some DOS games. Other DOS games will not run no matter how much coaxing you give them. DOS games tend to be very hardware-resource intensive. This is the primary reason that many game software developers write their programs to run in DOS. They like to have total control over the hardware — something that Windows 98 is not willing to give up.

My advice? Wait for the Windows 98 version of the game. Not an option? Okay, try running your program in a Windows DOS session. The following example supposes that you have a DOOM2 game located on your D drive in the \GAMES\DOOM2 directory:

> *1.* Click the Start button, highlight <u>P</u>rograms, and click MS-DOS Prompt.
>
> *2.* Switch to Full Screen mode by pressing Alt+Enter or clicking the Full Screen button.
>
> *3.* Type D: (don't forget the colon) and press Enter to select the D drive.
>
> *4.* Type CD \GAMES\DOOM2 and press Enter to change to the proper directory.
>
> *5.* Type DOOM2 and press Enter.

If that doesn't work, try running the game in MS-DOS mode (see the following section).

Running in MS-DOS mode

If you're sick of kowtowing to Windows 98 and want DOS to be boss, play your games (and, incidentally, do your work) in MS-DOS mode:

1. Click the Start button and choose Sh<u>u</u>t Down.

2. Click the Restart the computer in <u>M</u>S-DOS mode option.

3. Click the <u>O</u>K button.

4. Type D: and press Enter to select the D drive.

5. Type CD \GAMES\DOOM2 and press Enter to change to the proper directory.

6. Type DOOM2 and press Enter.

Although Windows 98 will be slower to start up the next time you turn on your computer, running in MS-DOS mode does no harm to your computer.

Customizing the DOS environment

You do have some control over the DOS environment in which you run your games. You access these controls through the Properties dialog box. You can start a DOS session for your game and change the properties for that session, but those properties will then apply to every DOS session that you start from then on — which may not be a great idea. You might want to create a shortcut icon instead (see the next section).

But you may want to adjust some of the following settings, which you can do in the Properties dialog box:

✦ Automatically run DOS full-screen.

✦ Automatically close the DOS window when a program is done.

✦ Change the DOS program icon.

✦ Enable or disable the screen saver when you're in DOS.

✦ Enable Windows key combinations in DOS.

✦ Have Windows remember your DOS settings (such as font size and window position).

✦ Change the title of the DOS program window.

 To access the Properties dialog box, click the Properties button on the DOS program's toolbar.

For more details, ***see also*** *DOS For Dummies,* 3rd Edition, Chapter 7.

Here's how to adjust some other settings for individual programs (create a shortcut icon for the program first — see "Creating shortcut icons" later in this part):

1. Open the Properties dialog box.

2. Click the Program tab.

3. Click the Ad<u>v</u>anced button.

The following configuration options are available in the Advanced Program Settings dialog box:

- **<u>P</u>revent MS-DOS–based programs from detecting Windows:** Some programs will not run if they detect that Windows is running. If this is the case with your program, click this check box.

- **Su<u>g</u>gest MS-DOS mode as necessary:** If you're not sure whether your program will run best in MS-DOS mode, click this check box.

- **<u>M</u>S-DOS mode:** If you know that your program will run best in MS-DOS mode, click this check box. Your check here will cause Windows 98 to close down all Windows and MS-DOS applications and attempt to give control of all system resources to this program.

If you click the check box next to MS-DOS mode, the following options become available:

- **<u>W</u>arn before entering MS-DOS mode:** Click this check box.

- **<u>U</u>se current MS-DOS configuration:** Try this setting first. If you find, after running the program, that this setting doesn't work, try the next one.

- **<u>S</u>pecify a new MS-DOS configuration:** Use this setting only if you know the changes to the CONFIG.SYS and AUTOEXEC.BAT files that the game software manufacturer suggests. This option is not for the technically timid.

4. Click the OK button in the next two dialog boxes.

5. Double-click your DOS program's shortcut icon.

Creating shortcut icons

Another way to customize Windows to make it more DOS-friendly is to create a shortcut icon on the desktop for each DOS game or program that you want to run, and change the properties associated with the individual shortcuts. Follow these steps to create a shortcut icon on the desktop (I've used DOOM2 as an example again):

1. Click the secondary mouse button (that's the right mouse button for most of you) on an empty part of the desktop.

2. Point to New.

3. Click Shortcut.

4. Type the full path and filename of your game in the Command line text box. For example:

D:\GAMES\DOOM2\DOOM2.EXE

If you're not sure of the full path and filename of your game, click the Browse button to navigate to the file.

5. Click Next.

6. Type a name for your shortcut or click Finish to accept the one that Windows 98 suggests.

Wasn't that fun? Use the same steps to create shortcuts to other DOS programs.

To change the properties for an individual shortcut, click the shortcut with the secondary mouse button and choose Properties from the context menu that appears. (See "Customizing the DOS environment" earlier in this part.)

Surviving DOS Commands

Now for some good news: Here's the list of DOS commands that made the transition to Windows 98, along with a brief description of each command. For more-detailed information, look up the command in the part specified in the following table.

Command	Brief Description	For More, See Part . . .
ATTRIB	Displays or changes file attributes	III
CHKDSK	Checks a disk and displays a status report (in Versions 6.2+, use ScanDisk instead)	III

Command	Brief Description	For More, See Part . . .
CHOICE	Waits for the user to select one of a set of choices	IV
DELTREE	Deletes a directory and all the subdirectories and files in it	III
DISKCOPY	Copies the contents of one floppy disk to another	III
DOSKEY	Edits command lines, recalls command lines, creates macros	III
EDIT	A text file editor	III
FC	Compares two files and displays the differences between them	III
FIND	Searches for a text string in a file or files	III
FORMAT	Formats a disk	III
LABEL	Creates, changes, or deletes the volume label of a disk	III
MEM	Displays the amount of used and free memory in your system	III
MODE	Configures system devices	III
MORE	Displays output one screen at a time	III
MOVE	Moves files and renames files and directories	III
SCANDISK	Checks for and fixes errors on disks	III
SHARE	Installs file sharing and locking capabilities on your hard disk	III
SORT	Sorts input and writes results to the screen, a file, or another device	III
SUBST	Associates a path with a drive letter	III
SYS	Copies MS-DOS system files and command interpreter to a disk	III
XCOPY	Copies files and directory trees	III

And here are some more commands that are still around but aren't covered in this book:

Command	Brief Description
DEBUG	A program-testing and -editing tool
EXTRACT	Extracts files from a cabinet file
FDISK	Configures a hard disk for use with MS-DOS
START	Runs a Windows-based program or an MS-DOS–based program
XCOPY32	Copies files and directory trees (New and Improved Version)

Salvagable DOS commands from the Windows 98 CD

You can get some of the old DOS commands back if you really want them. Microsoft was kind enough to include them on the Windows 98 CD. They're located in the \OTHER\OLDMSDOS directory. Don't have the CD version of Windows 98? Sorry, they're not included on the floppy disk version. The following table lists the old MS-DOS commands located on the Windows 98 CD. Most of them will run only in MS-DOS mode.

I advise you to stay away from all the italicized commands listed unless you really know what you're doing. Some of them can produce unexpected results (such as rebooting your PC), even in MS-DOS mode. The three that you might find helpful are shown in bold.

I've listed the extensions because you'll need them if you want to copy the command from the Windows 98 CD.

APPEND.EXE	**EXPAND.EXE**	*GRAPHICS.COM*
HELP.COM	*INTERLNK.EXE*	*INTERSVR.EXE*
LOADFIX.COM	*MEMMAKER.EXE*	*PRINT.EXE*
QBASIC.EXE	*REPLACE.EXE*	*RESTORE.EXE*
SIZER.EXE	*TREE.COM*	*UNDELETE.EXE*

Here's a little more information on the three useful commands that you can restore from the Windows 98 CD. Note that the first two have more than one file, as noted.

✦ **HELP:** HELP.COM and HELP.HLP. Provides MS-DOS command syntax and examples.

✦ **QBASIC:** QBASIC.COM and QBASIC.HLP. Lets you create programs with the QBasic programming environment or run programs that others have created with QBasic.

✦ **EXPAND:** Expands a compressed file. You can use this command to retrieve files from the MS-DOS setup disks. Compressed files that this command can retrieve have the extension ex_. This program does not work with the compressed files found on the Windows 98 CD or diskettes; those files have the extension cab.

Here's how to get the commands back. Keep in mind that many of the commands do not work properly or at all in Windows 98.

1. Put the Windows 98 CD in the CD-ROM drive.

2. At the DOS prompt, type D: and press Enter.

3. Type CD\OTHER\OLDMSDOS and press Enter.

4. Use the COPY command with the name of the command that you want to copy. Use the following format, substituting the appropriate command name for COMMAND.EXT:

```
COPY COMMAND.EXT C:\WINDOWS\COMMAND
```

5. Press Enter, and you're done.

Viruses

You have probably heard about computer viruses by now. If not, read on.

Feed a fever, delete a virus

Or is that feed a virus, delete a fever? I can never remember. Now, don't expect your computer to start sniffling any time soon. A computer virus is nothing more than a computer program. So what's all the hullabaloo? Well, these programs usually do something nasty, such as deleting your files or fouling up your computer's setup information. Some viruses are not dangerous, merely annoying. I recall a virus from a few years back that would display a message stating that your computer just got stoned. You would have to reboot to continue using your computer, but otherwise no harm was done.

"Well," you say, "I just won't put any of those virus programs on my computer!" The problem is that those nasty programmers (truly despicable creatures) who create those virus programs like to disguise them as legitimate programs. Some virus programs can attach themselves to other programs on your computer. In fact, most computers become infected by running a program that has been infected by a virus. Can you guess the best source of virus-infected files? Yep, the Internet!

By now, you are probably wondering how to protect your computer from the virus menace. The number one method of avoiding virus problems is knowing where your software comes from. I install software only from reputable sources. I buy only shrink-wrapped software and am very careful about what I download. I also use anti-virus software. Some paranoid types believe that the anti-virus software vendors are the ones creating the viruses in the first place. Personally, I don't believe it, but just because you're paranoid doesn't mean there isn't a virus out to get you.

Two of my favorite anti-virus programs are McAfee's VirusScan 3.0 and Symantec's Norton AntiVirus 4.0. You can buy the software at almost any store that sells computers. Alternatively, you may elect to download the software from the Internet. Be sure that you download the software from the McAfee (www.mcafee.com) or Symantec (www.symantec) corporate Web site and not some third party.

Anti-virus software vendors offer periodic updates to their programs. It is a good idea to get and install these updates so that your anti-virus program knows how to combat the latest viruses. Having an out-of-date anti-virus program may leave you unprotected.

Year 2000 Issues

You are using Windows 98 and are concerned about year 2000 issues. You don't know what all the fuss is about year 2000. Read on.

Will your computer explode on New Year's Day 2000? Just what you need — a hangover and sick computer. Don't worry, your computer will neither explode nor cease to function. Well, okay, it may cease to function, but not because of this date thing.

There are basically two types of year 2000 problems: BIOS problems and software date field problems.

Some PCs have a problem that resets the system date to 1980 when the the year 2000 arrives. This problem is caused by defects in the computer hardware and in the BIOS software.

The BIOS (Basic Input Output System) is software in a computer chip used to manage the low-level input and output functions of personal computer hardware. The operating system runs on top of the BIOS. That means that you tell the operating system what to do, and it in turn tells the BIOS what to do — which tells the computer hardware what to do.

How do you fix this problem? If you are running Windows 98, you don't have to do anything. Windows 98 automatically senses and corrects this problem.

Not running Windows 98? The easiest way to deal with this problem is to reset the date manually the first time you use your computer after January 1, 2000 using the DATE command. The syntax for the DATE command is:

```
DATE [month-day-year]
```

You can type DATE with no parameters to display the current date setting. If the system responds with a date of Tue 01-01-1980, enter the correct date after the Enter new date (mm-dd-yy) prompt.

The other type of year 2000 issue that you may encounter has to do with software written so long ago that the authors never dreamed anyone would still be using it in the year 2000. The authors either didn't allow dates past the year 2000 or limited the date field to two digits.

What should you do if you have a program that is not equipped to deal with the year 2000? Contact the manufacturer for an update, if available, or consider switching to a program that is year 2000 compliant.

IBM PC DOS users take note. The following programs do not process date information for years after 1999 correctly:

✦ Central Point Undelete for DOS

✦ Central Point Backup for DOS

✦ Central Point Backup for Windows

✦ REXX RXFINFO Utility

Download the Year 2000 Fix Pak from IBM at www.ibm.com/year2000 to correct these problems.

If you do not use these programs, you do not need to install this Fix Pak.

Part III

DOS Commands

If it just weren't for those darn DOS commands. . . .

In case you haven't already discovered this, you should know that DOS acts as though it were some kind of cantankerous genie who obeys your command only when you phrase it *exactly* the way he expects to hear it!

This "arrogance" means that to get anything useful done with DOS commands at the system prompt (that A> or C> thing), you have to watch your "p's and q's" and mind your spaces like a hawk. In this section, you'll find an alphabetical list of all the DOS commands, indicating what the command does along with what parameters it expects. This is what's commonly called *syntax* in other DOS books but what you and I know better as *DOSspeak*.

In addition to this kind of essential information, you can find out whether a command is one that *you* might actually use or one better left to the more serious (okay, *nerdy*) DOS user.

And watch out for Warning icons: remember, when used improperly, some commands can really mess with your computer.

In this part . . .

- ✔ **Manipulating drives, disks, directories, and files**
- ✔ **Backing up files**
- ✔ **Optimizing disk performance and space**
- ✔ **Getting help from DOS**
- ✔ **Using the DOS shell**
- ✔ **Watching out for viruses and bad disks**
- ✔ **Modifying hardware settings (keyboard, printer)**
- ✔ **. . . And much more!**

APPEND

Searches for data files in specified directories just as if they were in the current directory. Not included in the Windows 98 version of DOS.

APPEND pretty much does the job of the PATH command. You'll probably find PATH a lot easier to use.

DOSspeak

APPEND [/e][/x]

or

APPEND [[*drive:*][*path*[;...]] [/x [:on | :off]
    [/path:on | :off]

or

APPEND [;]

Variable or Option	Function
/e	(Versions 3.3+) Stores a copy of the appended search path in a DOS environment variable named APPEND. You must use this parameter the first time you give the APPEND command. Then give the APPEND command again, this time with the parameters specifying the appended search path.
/x	(Versions 3.3+) Extends the search path to include file searches and application execution. Enter this parameter only the first time that you use APPEND and before you enter the parameters of the search path.
/x:on	(Versions 4+) Same as /x except that you can use it any time you give the APPEND command.
/x:off	(Versions 4+) Turns off the extended search path initiated with the /x:on parameter so that DOS applies appended directories only to requests to open files (the default setting).
/path:on	(Versions 4+) Applies the appended directories to file requests that already include a path (the default setting).
/path:off	(Versions 4+) Turns off the /path:on (default) setting.
;	Separates search paths. When used alone, it cancels the search path previously set with APPEND.

If you enter APPEND with no other parameters, DOS just lists the current search path.

Sample

Say that you need to set the search path for data files to include the \STUFF and \NONSENSE directories on drive A as well as the \BALONEY directory on drive B. You enter

```
append a:\stuff;a:\nonsense;b:\baloney
```

ASSIGN

Reroutes requests for disk operations on one drive to another drive.

Note that the FORMAT, DISKCOPY, DISKCOMP, and SYS commands ignore any disk reassignments made with ASSIGN. Only use the ASSIGN command when you are running an older application that insists on using a particular floppy drive (especially if you don't have that drive).

DOSspeak

```
ASSIGN [x [:]=y[:][...]]
```

or

```
ASSIGN [/status]
```

Variable or Option	Function
x	Indicates the letter of the drive to be rerouted.
y	Indicates the letter of the drive that disk operations are rerouted to.
/status	(Versions 5+) Displays a report on the current drive assignments (can be abbreviated to /sta).

If you enter ASSIGN with no other parameters, DOS cancels any assignments currently in effect.

Sample

Say that you have a program that will look for data files only on drive B, but you happen to have only a floppy drive A and hard drive C. To instruct DOS to reroute all requests by the program for your nonexistent drive B to your hard drive C, you enter

```
assign b=c
```

If you have Version 4 or later, you can include the customary colons after the drive letters as follows:

```
assign b:=c:
```

ATTRIB

Displays or modifies the attributes of a file. These attributes include

+ ✦ Whether the file is read-only (so that it can't be tampered with)

+ ✦ Whether the file is marked with an archive flag (used by the BACKUP and XCOPY commands)

+ ✦ Whether the file is a system file

+ ✦ Whether the file is a hidden file

Be very stingy in your use of this command. There are usually good reasons that a file comes to you read-only, carries the archive flag, is a system file, or is currently hidden from directory listings.

DOSspeak

```
ATTRIB [+r | -r] [+a | -a] [+s | -s] [+h | -h]
       [drive:][path]filename [/s]
```

Variable or Option	Function
+r	Makes the file read-only so that you can't fool with it.
-r	Removes read-only status from the file so that you can fool with it.
+a	Sets the file's archive flag.
-a	Removes the file's archive flag.
+s	(Versions 5+) Sets the file's system flag.
-s	(Versions 5+) Removes the file's system flag.
+h	(Versions 5+) Hides the file so that it doesn't show up in a directory listing.
-h	(Versions 5+) Unhides the file so that it shows up in a directory listing again.
[drive:][path] filename	Specifies the drive, directory, and name of the file that has attributes you want to change. If the *drive:* and/or *path* parameters are omitted, DOS assumes that you mean the current drive and directory.
/s	Can be used when *filename* contains wildcard characters so that DOS processes matching files in all directories specified by the *path* parameter.

If you type *filename* after ATTRIB without using any other parameters, DOS displays the current attributes of that file.

Sample

Say that you're trying to delete an old version of a program from your hard disk to free some much needed space. However, you find that you just can't get rid of one file, RESISTS.DEL, in the current directory. To get its attribute status so that you can find out what the problem is, you enter

```
attrib resists.del
```

When you press Enter, DOS displays

```
R C:\RESISTS.DEL
```

telling you that this baby is read-only. To change the file's attribute to "you're dog meat if I say you are," you enter

```
attrib -r resists.del
```

BACKUP

Backs up files from one disk to another.

You must use the RESTORE command (rather than the regular COPY command) to put the files you backed up with the BACKUP command back onto their disks and directories.

Don't use the BACKUP command to back up files under the influence of the APPEND, ASSIGN, JOIN, or SUBST command.

DOSspeak

```
BACKUP source destination-drive: [/s] [/m] [/a]
    [/f:[size]] [/d:date] [/t:time]
    [/l[:[drive:][path]logfile]]
```

Variable or Option	Function
source	Specifies the file(s), drive, or directory that you want to back up.
destination-drive:	Specifies the drive with the destination disk where the backup files are saved.
/s	Backs up the contents of all subdirectories of the source path.
/m	Backs up only those files on the destination disk that have been modified since the last backup.
/a	Adds backup files to the destination disk (instead of replacing existing files, as is usually the case).

(continued)

Variable or Option	Function
/f:[size]	Formats the destination disk if it isn't already formatted. In Version 3.3, the /f switch has no size parameter. In Versions 4+, you must specify one of the following [size] parameters: 160K, 180K, 320K, 360K, 720K, 1.2MB, or 1.44MB.
/d:date	Backs up only those files changed on or after the specified date (*mm-dd-yy* is the default).
/t:time	Backs up only those files changed on or after the specified time (*hh:mm:ss* is the default).
/l[:[drive:][path]logfile]	Creates a log file with a list of all the files that were backed up. In Versions 3.2 and earlier, only the *logfile* parameter can be used (DOS automatically saves this file in the root directory of the destination disk). In Versions 4+, you can specify the pathname with the [*drive:*][*path*] parameters. If you don't specify a pathname, DOS uses the current directory. If you don't specify a filename, DOS names the file BACKUP.LOG.

Sample

Suppose that you need to back up all the files in your \MYTURF directory on drive C onto floppy disks in drive A (floppy disks that may or may not all be formatted). In that case, you enter

```
backup c:\myturf\*.* a:/f
```

CD or CHDIR

Displays or changes the current directory. CD is an abbreviated form of CHDIR. CHDIR does the same thing as CD and works the same way — its command name just requires more typing.

DOSspeak

```
CD [drive:][path]
```

Variable or Option	Function
drive:	Indicates the drive letter of the directory that you want to make current. Note that you can't use this parameter in the CD command to log on to a new drive; to do that, you simply enter the *drive:* parameter alone.
path	Indicates the name of the directory that you want to make current. When the *path* parameter includes one or more subdirectories, use the \ (backslash) to separate the directory names.

If you enter CD with no parameters, DOS displays the pathname of the current directory.

Sample

Suppose that you're in the root directory of drive C, and you want to work with some files in the \NONJUNK directory, which is a subdirectory of your C:\MYTURF directory. To do so, you enter

```
cd \myturf\nonjunk
```

After you're done fooling with the files in \NONJUNK, you can make \MYTURF the current directory by simply entering

```
cd..
```

(the two periods take you up to the next directory level). Finally, you're ready to leave \MYTURF and want to make the root directory of the hard disk current. To do so, you either enter cd.. again to move up one level, or you can specify the root directory by entering

```
cd\
```

CHCP

Displays or changes the code page number, which determines the character set that DOS uses to display and print characters.

DOSspeak

```
CHCP [nnn]
```

where *nnn* is a code page number as follows:

Code Page Number	Code Page Used
437	American (English)
850	Multilingual
860	Portuguese
863	French-Canadian
865	Nordic

If you omit the code page number parameter, DOS displays the current code page.

Sample

Say that Cousin Olaf comes to visit from Norway, and he wants to use your computer to write a letter back home. You can change the code page to Nordic by entering

```
chcp 865
```

Then, to make sure that both Olaf and your computer are now on the same code page, you can enter

```
chcp
```

and DOS displays

```
Active code page: 865
```

CHKDSK

Analyzes the allotment of storage on a disk and reports back on all kinds of interesting and not-so-interesting information, such as

✦ The disk's volume name and creation date

✦ The space occupied by different types of files and directories

✦ The number of bytes free and in bad sectors

✦ The total system memory

✦ A bunch of drivel about allocation units

Also reports on bits of fragmented files (known as *lost clusters in chains*) that are taking up space on the disk; you can remove these lost clusters or have them put into files.

You can't use CHKDSK on a drive under the influence of the ASSIGN, JOIN, or SUBST command, nor can you use it to check a drive on a network.

DOS 6.2+ users should use SCANDISK rather than CHKDSK.

DOSspeak

```
CHKDSK [drive:][path]filename [/v] [/f]
```

Variable or Option	Function
[drive:][path]	Specifies the drive and directory to check.
filename	Specifies the file(s) to check for fragmentation.

Variable or Option	Function
/v	Displays the pathname of each file as it checks it. Be aware that on a hard disk with hundreds of files, this is one *long* report!
/f	Converts lost clusters in chains to files with the extension CHK if you answer Y to the prompt. Removes the lost clusters if you answer N to the prompt.

If you enter CHKDSK with no parameters, DOS analyzes and reports on the entire drive to which you're logged.

Sample

Suppose that Al in Finance gives you a floppy disk, and you want to know whether it's a high-density disk and how much free space it has. With the disk in drive A, you enter

```
chkdsk a:
```

CLS

Clears your screen of everything but the ugly DOS prompt.

You can use the CLS command both at the DOS prompt and in batch files.

DOSspeak

```
CLS
```

Sample

To get rid of all those nasty DOS error messages that have filled the screen, you enter

```
cls
```

COMMAND

Starts a secondary instance of the command interpreter by loading another copy of the COMMAND.COM file.

See also EXIT.

WARNING!

If you ever do go so far as to actually use COMMAND to load a secondary DOS command interpreter (though why you would is unclear!), just be sure that you don't load any terminate-and-stay-resident (TSR) programs with the secondary interpreter; This miscalculation can lead to a crash that might result in data loss.

DOSspeak

```
COMMAND [[drive:]path] [device] [/c string]
    [/e:nnnnn] [/k filename] [/p] [/msg] [y]
```

Variable or Option	Function
[drive:]path	Specifies the pathname of the directory that contains the COMMAND.COM file.
device	Specifies a character device other than the standard keyboard and monitor used for input and output.
/c string	Instructs the secondary command interpreter to carry out the command specified by the *string* parameter and then automatically returns control to the parent command interpreter. When you are using this switch with other parameters, the /c switch must be the last one you enter.
/e:nnnnn	(Versions 3.2+) Specifies the size, in *nnnnn* bytes, of the environment block for the copy of the command interpreter.
/k filename	Specifies the program or batch file to run and then displays the DOS prompt.
/p	Disables the EXIT command, thereby making the secondary command interpreter permanent (that is, there's no escape back to the parent command interpreter until you restart the machine).
/msg	Specifies that all error messages be stored in memory (you need to use the /p switch in order to use this one).
/y	Instructs the secondary command interpreter to step line by line through the batch file specified by the /c or /k switch.

If you enter COMMAND with no parameters, DOS loads the secondary command interpreter and displays the version of DOS that you're using. To remove the secondary copy of the interpreter and return to the parent DOS interpreter, enter the EXIT command.

Sample

Suppose that you have a batch file called BUGHUNT.BAT, which you need to run with a secondary command interpreter (I know it's a stretch). To do something weird like this, you enter

```
command /c bughunt
```

COMP

Compares the contents of two files to determine whether they are identical. If they are identical, DOS indicates this with the message `Files compare OK`. If they aren't, DOS indicates the locations of the differences (as an offset from the beginning of the file) along with their mismatched bytes in (of all things) hexadecimal numbers.

DOSspeak

```
COMP [data1] [data2] [/d] [/a] [/l] [/n=number]
     [/c]
```

Variable or Option	Function
data1	(Versions 5+) Specifies the path and filename(s) of the first file(s) to be compared.
data2	(Versions 5+) Specifies the path and filename(s) of the file(s) to be compared with the first file(s).
/d	(Versions 5+) Displays differences as decimal numbers.
/a	(Versions 5+) Displays differences as ASCII characters.
/l	(Versions 5+) Displays the locations of differences by line number rather than offset.
/n=number	(Versions 5+) Specifies that only the number of lines in each file be compared.
/c	(Versions 5+) Disregards differences in uppercase and lowercase of ASCII characters when comparing files.

If you enter the COMP command with no parameters, DOS prompts you to enter the names of the files to be compared.

To compare specific sets of files to one another, use wildcard characters in the filenames that you enter for the [data1] and [data2] parameters. If you enter only pathnames for the [data1] and [data2] parameters, DOS compares all the files in the directories.

Sample

To determine whether the copy of the VITALDOC.TXT file on your floppy disk in drive A is identical to the original file in your \MYTURF directory, you enter

```
comp \myturf\vitaldoc.txt a:\vitaldoc.txt
```

COPY (Combine Files)

Combines two or more files into either the first file or a new file.

DOSspeak

```
COPY [source+source[+source]...] [destination] [/a]
     [/b] [/v] [/y | /-y]
```

Variable or Option	Function
source	Specifies the drives, directories, and names of the files to be combined. Instead of individually listing the filenames separated with + signs, you can use wildcard characters in the filenames.
destination	Specifies the directory and/or name for the new file containing the combined data of the source files. If you omit the destination parameter, DOS combines all the source files in the series into the first source file listed in the command.
/a	Indicates that the source and/or destination files are ASCII (text) files.
/b	Indicates that the source and/or destination files are binary files.
/v	Verifies that the contents of the new destination file match the combined contents of the source files from which the destination file is created.
/y	Indicates that you want COPY to replace existing file(s) without prompting you for confirmation.
/-y	Makes COPY prompt you for confirmation when replacing an existing file.

Remember: The /a and /b switches affect the filename that immediately precedes them in the command line as well as any filenames that follow them — until DOS encounters another /a or /b switch.

Sample

Suppose that you want to join a file called BUNK.DOC with another called HOOEY.DOC into a new third document, which is to be called TWADDLE.DOC. To do so, you enter

```
copy bunk.doc+hooey.doc twaddle.doc
```

COPY (Device to Device or File)

Copies the output of a device to a file or another device.

When sending output from one device to another device or to a file, be sure that you don't mess up and specify a device that you don't own (or mistype the name of a device that you do actually have). This mistake has been known to throw DOS for a loop and could crash your computer.

DOSspeak

```
COPY source destination
```

Variable or Option	Function
source	Specifies the name of the device whose output you want to copy.
destination	Specifies the file or device to which the output of the source device is to be copied. If destination is a file, you can include the path but no wildcard characters.

Sample

To copy what you type at the keyboard into a file named FASTNOTE.TXT, you enter

```
copy con fastnote.txt
```

If you want to send what you type directly to the printer rather than to a file, you enter

```
copy con prn
```

In both cases, when you've finished typing, you need to press Ctrl+Z or F6 and then press Enter to terminate the COPY command.

COPY (File to Device)

Copies a file to a device, such as your printer.

When sending a file to a device, such as your printer or the screen, be aware that if you mistype the name of the device, the computer may freeze up on you, forcing you to reset it.

DOSspeak

```
COPY source [/a] [/b] device
```

Variable or Option	Function
source	Specifies the path and name of the file whose output you want to copy to the device.
/a	Indicates that the *source* file is an ASCII (text) file.
/b	Indicates that the *source* file is a binary file.
device	Specifies the device to which the output of the *source* file is to be copied.

Sample

To send a copy of a file named README.TXT to your printer, you enter

```
copy readme.txt prn
```

To send the same file to the screen, you enter

```
copy readme.txt con
```

COPY (File to File)

Copies a file to another file, or a group of files to another group of files.

 If the *source* and *destination* parameters indicate the same file in the same location on a disk, you'll get an error message indicating that DOS is completely faked out because the file cannot be copied onto itself.

 Although COPY is usually a pretty user-friendly command, you can get yourself into trouble if you mistakenly specify an existing filename as the *destination* file whose data you don't really want replaced by the *source* file. Keep in mind that if the *destination* file exists, COPY replaces it with the *source* file information without asking you for any confirmation, and DOS provides *no way* to undo this type of boo-boo!

DOSspeak

```
COPY source destination [/a] [/b] [/v]
```

Variable or Option	Function
source	Specifies the directory and name of the file(s) to be copied.
destination	Specifies the directory and/or name for the new files.

Variable or Option	Function
/a	Indicates that the *source* and/or *destination* files are ASCII (text) files.
/b	Indicates that the *source* and/or *destination* files are binary files.
/v	Verifies that the new *destination* files match the *source* files from which they are copied.

Remember: The /a and /b switches affect the filename that immediately precedes them in the command line as well as any filenames that follow them — until DOS encounters another /a or /b switch.

Sample

Suppose that Al in Finance needs a copy of your worksheet, FORECAST.WK1, that's in the \123STUFF directory on your drive C. Currently, you're logged on to the root directory of drive C and have Al's floppy disk in drive A. To make a copy of the worksheet to his floppy disk, you enter

```
copy \123stuff\forecast.wk1 a:
```

Now suppose that you're already logged on to your \123STUFF directory, and you want to copy all your worksheets to a directory called \MYMESSES. This time, you need to enter

```
copy *.wk1 c:\mymesses
```

CTTY

Reroutes console input and output to a hardware device, such as the COM1 or COM2 communications port.

 This command is safe only in the hands of a programmer or some other totally DOSsed person. Stay clear unless they give you hazard pay.

DOSspeak

```
CTTY device
```

where *device* is a valid hardware device such as COM1 or AUX.

Sample

To reroute the input and output through the COM1 communications port, you enter

```
ctty com1
```

To once again route input and output through keyboard and screen, you enter

```
ctty con
```

Remember: The latter command must be sent via the COM1 port — you can't just type it from the keyboard, because the keyboard is no longer the computer's input device!

DATE

Displays or sets the date used by DOS and application programs to add the date stamp to files.

Even though DOS doesn't tell you, it *will* accept a date separated with slashes rather than dashes — such as 2/15/97 rather than 2-15-97. Also, even though DOS *shows* you the day of the week preceding the date when you use the DATE command, DOS won't accept an entry of anything but the actual date. Finally, if someone has fooled around with the COUNTRY command, you may have to vary the date format to something like 15-2-97 (for February 15, 1997).

DOSspeak

```
DATE [month-day-year]
```

Variable or Option	Function
month	Specifies the *month* as a number between 1 and 12.
day	Specifies the *day* as a number between 1 and 31 (no need to include leading zeros, such as 01).
year	Specifies the *year* in the 20th century as a number between 80 and 99 (for dates in the 21st century, enter all four digits of the year, such as 2001).

You can type DATE with no parameters to display the current date setting.

Sample

To see what day your computer thinks it is, you enter

```
date
```

and press Enter at the `Enter new date (mm-dd-yy)` prompt. Suppose that today is really May Day, 1996, but DOS still thinks it's April Fool's Day. To set the date straight, you type

```
date 5-1-96
```

and press Enter.

DEFRAG

Reorganizes the files on a disk to optimize disk performance (available only in DOS 6+).

Entering the DEFRAG command from the DOS prompt under Windows 95 or later launches the Windows Disk Defragmenter program.

Be aware that optimizing a large hard disk is a time-consuming process. Therefore, you may want to enter the DEFRAG command right before you leave the office so that DEFRAG can optimize your disk overnight.

DOSspeak

```
DEFRAG [drive:] [/f] [/s[:]order] [/b] [skiphigh]
    [lcd | /bw | /g0] [/h]
```

or

```
DEFRAG [drive:] [/u] [/b] [/skiphigh] [lcd | /bw |
    /g0] [/h]
```

Variable or Option	Function
drive:	Specifies the drive with the disk you want to optimize.
/f	Ensures that there are no empty spaces between files when defragmenting a disk.
/u	Leaves the empty spaces between files when defragmenting a disk.
/s[:]order	Sorts files in their directories according to the *order* parameter when defragmenting a disk. The order parameter can be any of the following values: n (for alphabetical order by filename), n- (for reverse alphabetical order by filename), e (for alphabetical order by extension), e- (for reverse alphabetical order by extension), d (for date and time order, least recent to most recent), d- (for date and time order, most recent to least recent), s (for size order, smallest to largest), or s- (for size order, largest to smallest). When combining *order* parameters, don't separate them with spaces.
/b	Reboots your computer as soon as DEFRAG finishes optimizing your drive.
/skiphigh	Loads DEFRAG into conventional memory rather than upper memory (as is usually the case when sufficient upper memory is available).

(continued)

Variable or Option	Function
/lcd	Displays the DEFRAG screen in an LCD color scheme.
/bw	Displays the DEFRAG screen in a black-and-white color scheme.
/g0	Disables the graphics character set and the graphical mouse pointer in the DEFRAG screen.
/h	Moves hidden files when defragmenting a disk.

If you enter DEFRAG with nono parameters, DOS loads DEFRAG and displays the DEFRAG screen, using the default display values.

Sample

To optimize drive C and sort the files in date-and-time order (most recent to least recent), you enter

```
defrag c: /f /sd-
```

DEL or ERASE

Deletes one or more files from your disk.

The DEL and ERASE commands are identical in purpose (obviously, they differ in name). Also, if you like to do more typing, you can type DELETE rather than DEL.

Unless you are using DOS Version 5 or later, or have a fancy DOS utility that can bring deleted files back from the dead, all deletions made with ERASE or DEL are final. Therefore, *before* you enter this command, be sure that

✦ You're in the right directory — *see* DIR.

✦ You've typed the right path and filename(s).

✦ You've got the files backed up on another disk (unless they're just complete garbage) — *see* BACKUP and the COPY commands.

DOSspeak

```
DEL [drive:][path]filename [/p]
```

or

```
ERASE [drive:][path]filename [/p]
```

Variable or Option	Function
[*drive:*][*path*]*filename*	Specifies the drive, directory, and names of the file(s) to be erased. If the *drive:* and/or *path* parameters are omitted, DOS assumes that you want to use the current drive and directory.
	You can use wildcard characters to delete a group of files, but beware of the *.* wildcard combination because, used with this command, it will erase all files in the current directory.
/p	(Versions 4+) Specifies that DOS should prompt you before deleting each file.

Sample

To delete the file named GARBAGE.DOC in your C:\MYJUNK directory when the root directory on drive C is current, you enter

```
del \myjunk\garbage.doc
```

To delete all the files in your \MYJUNK directory that use the file extension CRP, when the \MYJUNK directory is current, you enter

```
erase *.crp
```

DELTREE

Deletes a directory and all the files and subdirectories in it (available only in DOS 6+).

Be careful with the DELTREE command because it deletes *all* files in the specified directory or subdirectories regardless of their attributes — including files marked with the read-only, hidden, and system attributes. *See* ATTRIB for more on these attributes.

DOSspeak

```
DELTREE [/y] [drive:]path
```

Variable or Option	Function
/y	Deletes all the files and subdirectories in the specified directory without prompting you for confirmation (a potentially dangerous switch).
[*drive:*]*path*	Specifies the drive and directory whose files and subdirectories are to be deleted.

Sample

To delete all the files and subdirectories in your \MYJUNK directory (including the two subdirectories \HOTTRASH and \RUBBISH), you enter

```
deltree c:\myjunk
```

DIR

Displays a list of all the files and subdirectories in a directory.

DOSspeak

```
DIR [drive:][path][filename] [/p] [/w]
    [/a[[:]attributes]] [/o[[:]sortorder]] [/s]
    [/b] [/l] [/c[h]]
```

Variable or Option	Function
[drive:][path][filename]	Specifies the drive, directories, or files to include in the directory listing.
/p	Pauses the directory listing after each screen of information and displays the message Press any key to continue.
/w	Displays the directory listing in a wide format of five columns across the screen. In the wide format in Versions 5+, the names of subdirectories are enclosed in square brackets, such as [MYTURF].
/a:attributes	(Versions 5+) Restricts the directory listing to just those entries with the particular attribute parameter.
	Attribute parameters include a for Archive, d for directory, h for hidden, r for read-only, and s for system files.
	To exclude particular attributes from a directory listing, preface the *attribute* parameter with a dash (hyphen), such as dir /a:-s to eliminate all system files from the directory listing.
	If you use the /a switch with no no *attribute* parameter, DOS displays all entries, including hidden and system files.
/o:sortorder	(Versions 5+) Specifies the sort order in which entries are displayed in the directory listing.
	Sortorder parameters include n for alphabetical order by filename, e for alphabetical order by extension, s for ascending order by size (smallest to largest), d for ascending order by date and time (oldest to newest), or g to place subdirectories ahead of files in the list.

Variable or Option	Function
	To reverse the sort order (display the files in order of largest to smallest), preface the *sortorder* parameter with a dash (hyphen), such as dir /o:-s.
	If you use the /o switch with no no *sortorder* parameter, DOS sorts the entries by name and places subdirectories ahead of files.
/	(Versions 5+) Displays files in the directory specified by the *path* parameter *and* the files in all its subdirectories.
/b	(Versions 5+) Displays the directory listing in a bare-bones format, without the size and revision date and time information, or the summary information.
/l	(Versions 5+) Displays all file and subdirectory names in lowercase letters.
/c[h]	(Versions 6.0 and 6.2+) Displays the compression ratio of files compressed with DoubleSpace or DriveSpace, based on an 8K cluster size. The optional h parameter displays the compression ratio based on the cluster size of the host drive. The h parameter is ignored when used with the /w or /b switch.

If you enter DIR with no parameters, DOS lists all files and subdirectories of the current directory in one blur.

Sample

Suppose that you're in your \MYTURF directory and you want a wide listing of all the files without listing any of the subdirectories, such as \MYMESSES. You enter

```
dir /w /a:-d
```

Now you decide that you want to see all the files in this directory in descending order of their revision date and time (newest to oldest). Because you have so much junk in this directory, you also want DOS to pause at each screenful. To do so, you enter

```
dir /p /o:-d
```

DISKCOMP

Compares the contents of two floppy disks track by track and, if the disks are not identical, reports on which tracks are different.

Note: You can't use DISKCOMP to compare disks of different types, such as a double-sided 360K disk with a high-density 1.2MB disk.

Also, don't try using DISKCOMP with a drive under the influence of the JOIN or ASSIGN commands (but, then again, why are you using DISKCOMP at all?).

DOSspeak

```
DISKCOMP [drive1: [drive2:]] [/1] [/8]
```

Variable or Option	Function
drive1:	Specifies the drive containing the first floppy disk to be compared.
drive2:	Specifies the drive containing the second floppy disk to be compared.
/l	Restricts the disk comparison to just the first side of the floppy disks even when the disks are double-sided.
/8	Limits the disk comparison to the first 8 sectors per track even if the first floppy disk has 9 or even 15 sectors per track.

Note: If you omit the *drive2:* parameter, DOS compares the floppy disk specified with *drive1:* to the disk in the current floppy drive (make sure that you're not logged on to the hard drive). If you omit both drive parameters, DOS assumes that you want to use *only* the current floppy drive when comparing disks (useful if you have only a drive A) and prompts you to insert the different disks.

Sample

Suppose that you've got nothing better to do and you're dying to verify that the copy of the floppy disk that you just made with DISKCOPY for Al in Finance is identical to your original floppy disk. To do so, you make drive A current by typing

```
a:
```

and pressing Enter. Then you enter

```
diskcomp
```

Next, in response to the prompt Insert FIRST diskette in drive A:, you put the original floppy disk in drive A and press Enter. When prompted by DOS with Insert SECOND diskette in drive A:, you replace the original disk with Al's copy in drive A and press Enter. Then, you press N when DOS asks whether you want to compare another disk (you do have *useful* work to do, don't you?)

DISKCOPY

Duplicates one floppy disk on another floppy disk of the same type.

Note: You can't use DISKCOPY to copy a disk of a different type — for example, a double-sided 360K disk onto a high-density 1.2MB disk.

DOSspeak

```
DISKCOPY [drive1: [drive2:]] [/1] [/v] [/m]
```

Variable or Option	Function
drive1:	Specifies the drive containing the floppy disk to be copied.
drive2:	Specifies the drive containing the floppy disk where the duplicate is to be made.
/l	Duplicates only the first side of the floppy disk in *drive1:* even when the disk is double-sided.
/v	(Versions 5+) Verifies that the duplicates are identical (making the aforementioned DISKCOMP command superfluous).
/m	Forces DISKCOPY to use only conventional memory for an interim storage area when copying one floppy to another. (DOS 6.2+ uses the hard drive as an interim storage area.)

Note: If you omit the *drive2:* parameter, DOS copies the floppy disk specified with *drive1:* onto the disk in the current floppy drive (make sure that you're not logged on to the hard disk). If you omit both drive parameters, DOS assumes that you want to use *only* the current floppy drive when duplicating disks (useful if you have only a drive A) and prompts you to insert the different disks.

Sample

Suppose that you need to make a duplicate of a floppy disk for Al in Finance. You put your original floppy disk in drive A and an unformatted floppy disk in drive B; then, you enter

```
diskcopy a: b: /v
```

Now, suppose that today you're working on Sue's machine, and her old klunker has only one floppy drive. To make another copy of your floppy disk for Al, this time you put your original in Sue's floppy drive, type

```
a:
```

and press Enter to log on to drive A. Then type

```
diskcopy
```

Press Enter at the prompt Insert SOURCE diskette in drive A: to start the copy process and then replace the original floppy disk with the new unformatted floppy disk when you see the Insert TARGET diskette in drive A: prompt. Press Enter to start the copy. You follow the prompts, switching to the original disk when prompted for the SOURCE disk and to the duplicate disk when prompted for the TARGET disk.

DOSHELP

Displays an alphabetical list of all DOS and batch commands or a short description of a particular command (including the DOSspeak line and a listing of the parameters). For Versions 6.0 to 6.22, *see* HELP.

DOSspeak

DOSHELP [*command*]

where *command* is the name of the DOS command you want help information on. If you enter DOSHELP without entering a command, DOS displays a quick list of all the DOS commands.

Sample

Al in Finance has borrowed your copy of *DOS For Dummies Quick Reference,* 3rd Edition, and you need information right now on how to back up all the files in your \MYTURF directory that have been modified since last December. To display help on the BACKUP command in the hope that you get these backups made before next December, you enter

```
doshelp backup
```

DOSKEY

Installs a DOSKEY utility that lets you recall previously used DOS commands to the command line, edit DOS commands on the command line with the left arrow (←) and right arrow (→) keys before you enter the commands, and create macros that play back DOS commands (DOSKEY is available in Versions 5+ only).

DOSspeak

```
DOSKEY [/reinstall] [/bufsize=size] [/macros]
    [/history] [/insert] [/overstrike]
    [macroname=[text]]
```

Variable or Option	Function
/reinstall	Installs a new copy of DOSKEY into memory, wiping out any commands or macros currently in memory.
/bufsize=size	Specifies the size in bytes of the area in memory (called a buffer) where DOSKEY stores your commands and macros (the default is 512 bytes). You can use this switch only when you first start or reinstall DOSKEY.
/macros	Displays all DOSKEY macros currently in the DOSKEY buffer.
/history	Displays all DOS commands currently in the DOSKEY buffer.
/insert	Puts DOSKEY in Insert mode so that new characters are inserted into the old text.
/overstrike	Puts DOSKEY in Overtype mode so that new characters replace old text (this is the default).
macroname	Specifies the name for a macro that you want to record.
text	Specifies the DOS commands that you want to record in your macro.

Sample

To install DOSKEY so that you can edit DOS commands with the arrow keys as well as recall previously used commands to the command line with the arrow keys, you enter

```
doskey
```

After installing DOSKEY, you can use the ↑ and ↓ keys to move up and down through the DOS commands you've used since you started DOSKEY. To edit a DOS command, use the ← and → keys to move the cursor to the characters that need editing. To display a numbered list of all the DOS commands in memory, press F7. To select a command by number, press F9 and then enter its number. To clear the DOSKEY buffer of all DOS commands, press Alt+F7.

DOSSHELL

Starts the DOS shell, a menu-driven utility that enables you to perform many basic DOS tasks without ever having to type a single one of these awful DOS commands (sorry, folks, this utility is available only for Versions 4 to 6.1).

DOSspeak

```
DOSSHELL [/t[:res[n]]] [/b]
```

or

```
DOSSHELL [/g[:res[n]]] [/b]
```

Variable or Option	Function
/t	Starts the DOS shell in text mode.
/g	Starts the DOS shell in graphics mode.
:res[n]	Specifies the screen resolution that the DOS shell is to use. The n parameters include l for low resolution, m for medium, and h for high resolution.
/b	Forces the DOS shell to be displayed in monochrome on a color monitor (use this switch to increase the screen contrast on a laptop that normally uses shades of gray to represent colors).

Sample

To start the DOS shell program from the DOS prompt, you type

```
dosshell
```

When you've finished having fun in the DOS shell and are ready to get back to reality at the DOS prompt, press Alt+F4 or Alt+F, X to quit the DOS shell.

DRVSPACE (Check Disk)

Checks a compressed floppy or hard disk for errors, such as lost clusters or cross-linked files. In DOS 6.22+, DriveSpace replaces the utility that's known as DoubleSpace in Versions 6.0 and 6.20 (no disk compression utility is included with MS-DOS 6.21 and versions prior to 6.0).

DOS 6.2+ replaces this command with SCANDISK.

Entering the DRVSPACE command from the DOS prompt under Windows 95 or later launches the Windows Drive Space utility.

When using this command, be careful that you don't accidentally delete any files that you really want to keep.

DOSspeak

DRVSPACE [/chkdsk] [/f] [*drive:*]

Variable or Option	Function
/chkdsk	Instructs the DriveSpace program to check the structural integrity of a compressed disk (you can abbreviate it to /chk).
/f	Fixes errors on the compressed disk.
drive:	Specifies the drive with the compressed disk that you want checked. If you omit this parameter, DOS assumes that you have selected the current drive.

If you enter DRVSPACE with no parameters, DOS starts the DriveSpace program, in which you can use menu options to check the compressed disk.

Sample

To check drive C after you've compressed it, you enter

drvspace /chkdsk c:

DRVSPACE (Compress)

Compresses a floppy or hard disk to free more space. In DOS 6.22+, DriveSpace replaces the utility that's known as DoubleSpace in Versions 6.0 and 6.20 (no disk compression utility is included with MS-DOS 6.21 and versions prior to 6.0).

To compress your startup hard disk, you must have at least 1.7MB of space free. To compress other hard disks, you need at least 1MB of free space. To compress floppy disks, you must have at least 200K of free space (you can't compress 360K floppies).

This command is safe only in the hands of a programmer or some other totally DOSsed person. Stay clear unless they give you hazard pay.

DOSspeak

DRVSPACE [/compress] *drive1:* [/newdrive=*drive2:*]
    [/reserve=*size*] [/f]

Variable or Option	Function
/compress	Tells DOS to compress the specified disk (you can abbreviate this switch to /com).
drive1:	Specifies the existing drive containing the disk you want to compress.
/newdrive=*drive2*	Specifies the drive letter for the uncompressed (host) drive. When DriveSpace compresses an existing drive, your system includes both the existing (compressed) drive and a new (uncompressed) drive. If you omit the /newdrive switch, DriveSpace assigns the next available drive letter. (You can abbreviate the /newdrive switch to /new.)
/reserve=*size*	Specifies how many megabytes (MB) of space to leave uncompressed for files that don't work correctly when compressed, such as the Windows swap file. The uncompressed space reserved with this switch resides on the new (uncompressed) drive. (You can abbreviate this switch to /res.)
/f	Suppresses the display of the final screen of statistics.

If you enter DRVSPACE alone, DOS starts the DriveSpace program, in which you can use the menu options to compress your disk.

Sample

To compress your hard disk on drive C, make drive D the new (uncompressed) drive, and reserve 2MB of uncompressed space on this new disk, you enter

```
drvspace /compress c: /new=d: /res=2
```

DRVSPACE (Create)

Creates a new compressed drive by using free space on an uncompressed drive. In DOS 6.22+, DriveSpace replaces the utility that's known as DoubleSpace in Versions 6.0 and 6.20 (no disk compression utility is included with MS-DOS 6.21 and versions prior to 6.0).

DOSspeak

```
DRVSPACE [/create] [drive1:] [/newdrive=drive2:]
    [/size=size | /reserve=size]
```

Variable or Option	Function
/create	Creates the new compressed drive, using the uncompressed drive specified by the *drive1:* parameter. (You can abbreviate this switch to /c.)
drive1:	Specifies the uncompressed drive whose space is to be used in creating the new compressed drive.
/newdrive=*drive2:*	Specifies the letter of the new compressed drive that you are creating. If you omit the /newdrive switch, DOS assigns the next available drive. (You can abbreviate this switch to /n.)
/size=*size*	Specifies the amount of space (in megabytes) on the uncompressed drive that you want to allocate to the compressed drive. You can't use the /size switch with the /reserve switch (see next option). (You can abbreviate this switch to /si.)
/reserve=*size*	Specifies how much free space (in megabytes) DriveSpace should leave on the uncompressed drive. To make the compressed drive as big as possible, specify 0 as the *size* parameter. You can't use the /reserve switch with the /size switch. If you omit both switches, DriveSpace reserves 2MB of free space. (You can abbreviate this switch to /re.)

If you enter DRVSPACE alone, DOS starts the DriveSpace program, in which you can use the menu options to create a new compressed disk.

DRVSPACE (Defragment)

Defragments a compressed disk by consolidating its free space. In DOS 6.22+, DriveSpace replaces the utility that's known as DoubleSpace in Versions 6.0 and 6.20 (no disk compression utility is included with MS-DOS 6.21 and versions prior to 6.0).

 If you intend to further compress a compressed drive — *see* DRVSPACE (Compress) — you should first consolidate the free space with the DRVSPACE /DEFRAGMENT command.

DOSspeak

```
DRVSPACE [/defragment] [drive:] [/f]
```

Variable or Option	Function
/defragment	Tells the DriveSpace program to consolidate all free space on the compressed disk specified by the *drive:* parameter. (You can abbreviate this switch to /def.)
drive:	Specifies the compressed disk to defragment.
/f	Enables the drive to be defragmented more fully.

If you enter DRVSPACE alone, DOS starts the DriveSpace program, in which you can use the menu options to defragment a compressed disk.

Sample

To defragment your compressed hard disk (drive C), you enter

```
drvspace /def c:
```

DRVSPACE (Delete)

Deletes a compressed drive and all the files on it. In DOS 6.22+, DriveSpace replaces the utility that's known as DoubleSpace in Versions 6.0 and 6.20 (no disk compression utility is included with MS-DOS 6.21 and versions prior to 6.0).

If you delete a compressed disk by mistake, you may be able to restore it. First, use the UNDELETE command to restore the deleted compressed volume file (using a filename such as DRVSPACE.*xxx,* such as DRVSPACE.001). After undeleting this file, use the DRVSPACE /MOUNT command to mount the file again — *see* DRVSPACE (Mount).

This command is safe only in the hands of a programmer or some other totally DOSsed person. Stay clear unless they give you hazard pay.

DOSspeak

```
DRVSPACE [/delete] [drive:]
```

Variable or Option	Function
/delete	Tells the DriveSpace program to delete all the files on the compressed disk specified by the *drive:* parameter. (You can abbreviate this switch to /del.)
drive:	Specifies which compressed disk to delete (DriveSpace won't let you delete drive C, however).

If you enter DRVSPACE alone, DOS starts the DriveSpace program, in which you can use the menu options to delete a compressed disk.

DRVSPACE (DoubleGuard)

Enables or disables DoubleGuard. Enabled, DriveSpace checks its memory, looking for damage from another program and preventing lots of data loss by stopping the computer when it finds damage. Note that you must restart your computer to make this switch work. In DOS 6.22+, DriveSpace replaces the utility that's known as DoubleSpace in Versions 6.0 and 6.20 (no disk compression utility is included with MS-DOS 6.21 and versions prior to 6.0).

This command is safe only in the hands of a programmer or some other totally DOSsed person. Stay clear unless they give you hazard pay.

DOSspeak

```
DRVSPACE [/doubleguard=0 | 1]
```

Variable or Option	Function
0	Keeps DriveSpace from looking for damage in its memory.
1	Tells DriveSpace to look for damage in its memory.

DRVSPACE (Format)

Formats a compressed disk (available only in DOS 6+).

Be careful. This command completely deletes all the drive's compressed data, just as the standard FORMAT wipes out all existing data on an uncompressed drive.

DOSspeak

```
DRVSPACE [/format] [drive:]
```

Variable or Option	Function
/format	Tells the DriveSpace program to format the compressed disk specified by the *drive:* parameter. (You can abbreviate this switch to /f.)
drive:	Specifies the compressed disk to format.

If you enter DRVSPACE alone, DOS starts the DriveSpace program, in which you can use the menu options to format a compressed disk.

DRVSPACE (Info)

Displays lots of useful information about a compressed drive, including the drive's used and free space, the name of its compressed volume, and its compression ratios. In DOS 6.22+, DriveSpace replaces the utility that's known as DoubleSpace in Versions 6.0 and 6.20 (no disk compression utility is included with MS-DOS 6.21 and versions prior to 6.0).

DOSspeak

```
DRVSPACE [/info] [drive:]
```

Variable or Option	Function
/info	Tells the DriveSpace program to give you information on the compressed disk specified by the *drive:* parameter. You can omit this switch altogether as long as you specify the *drive:* parameter.
drive:	Specifies the compressed disk that you want information on.

If you enter DRVSPACE alone, DOS starts the DriveSpace program, in which you can use the menu options to get information about a compressed disk.

Sample

To get information on your compressed hard disk (drive C), you enter

```
drvspace /info c:
```

You can also enter this command simply as

```
drvspace c:
```

DRVSPACE (List)

Lists all your computer's drives (except for network drives) with a brief description. In DOS 6.22+, DriveSpace replaces the utility that's known as DoubleSpace in Versions 6.0 and 6.20 (no disk compression utility is included with MS-DOS 6.21 and versions prior to 6.0).

DOSspeak

```
DRVSPACE [/list]
```

where /list tells DriveSpace to display a listing of local (non-network) drives on your computer (you may abbreviate this switch to /l). If you enter DRVSPACE alone, DOS starts the DriveSpace program, in which you can use the menu options to list your local drives.

Sample

To get a list of all the compressed and uncompressed local drives on your computer, you enter

```
drvspace /list
```

DRVSPACE (Mount)

Establishes a connection between a compressed volume file (CVF) and a drive letter so that you can use the files in this compressed volume file. You must mount a CVF only when you've previously unmounted it with the DRVSPACE /unmount switch or when the CVF is on a floppy disk. In DOS 6.22+, DriveSpace replaces the utility that's known as DoubleSpace in Versions 6.0 and 6.20 (no disk compression utility is included with MS-DOS 6.21 and versions prior to 6.0).

DOSspeak

```
DRVSPACE [/mount[=nnn]] [drive1:]
    [/newdrive=drive2:]
```

Variable or Option	Function
/mount[=nnn]	Mounts the compressed volume file with the extension specified by the nnn parameter. If you omit the nnn parameter, DriveSpace mounts the CVF named DRVSPACE.000. (You can enter the /mount switch as /mo.)
drive1:	Specifies the drive that contains the compressed volume file (CVF) that you want to mount. You must supply this parameter when using the /mount switch.
/newdrive=drive2:	Specifies the drive letter that you want assigned to the newly mounted CVF. If you omit this parameter, DriveSpace uses the next available drive letter. (You can abbreviate this switch to /new.)

If you enter DRVSPACE alone, DOS starts the DriveSpace program, in which you can use menu options to mount a compressed volume file.

Sample

To mount a compressed floppy disk in drive A, you enter

```
drvspace /mount a:
```

DRVSPACE (Ratio)

Modifies the compression ratio that estimates how much free space is available on a compressed drive. In DOS 6.22+, DriveSpace replaces the utility that's known as DoubleSpace in Versions 6.0 and 6.20 (no disk compression utility is included with MS-DOS 6.21 and versions prior to 6.0).

Each time you start your computer, DriveSpace adjusts the estimated compression ratio to match the average compression ratio of the files currently stored on that compressed drive.

DOSspeak

```
DRVSPACE /ratio[=r.r] [drive: | /all]
```

Variable or Option	Function
/ratio[=r.r]	Changes the estimated compression ratio for the compressed drive specified by the *drive:* or /all parameter to the ratio specified by the *r.r* parameter (between 1.0 and 16.0). If you omit the *r.r* parameter, DriveSpace sets the drive's estimated compression ratio to the actual average ratio for all the files on the specified drive. (You can abbreviate this switch to /ra.)
drive:	Specifies the letter of the compressed drive whose estimated compression ratio is to be tweaked. If you don't use this parameter or the /all switch, DriveSpace changes the ratio for the current drive.
/all	Changes the estimated compression ratio for all the mounted compressed drives. You can't use this switch with the *drive:* parameter.

If you enter DRVSPACE alone, DOS starts the DriveSpace program, in which you can use menu options to change the compression ratio for a compressed drive.

Sample

To increase the drive C estimated compression ratio to 8 to 1, you enter

```
drvspace /ratio=8 c:
```

DRVSPACE (Size)

Changes the size of a compressed drive. In DOS 6.22+, DriveSpace replaces the utility that's known as DoubleSpace in Versions 6.0 and 6.20 (no disk compression utility is included with MS-DOS 6.21 and versions prior to 6.0).

This command is safe only in the hands of a programmer or some other totally DOSsed person. Stay clear unless they give you hazard pay.

DOSspeak

DRVSPACE [/size[=*size1* | /reserve=*size2*]] [*drive:*]

Variable or Option	Function
/size=*size1*	Changes the size of the compressed drive specified by the *drive:* parameter to the size specified by the *size1* parameter. The *size1* parameter is the number of megabytes of space that this drive's compressed volume file occupies on the uncompressed (host) drive.
	You can specify the new size with either the /size or /reserve switch (see the following option) but not with both. If you omit both switches, DriveSpace makes the specified drive as small as possible. (You can abbreviate the /size switch to /si.)
/reserve=*size2*	Specifies the free space (in megabytes) that you want the uncompressed (host) drive to retain after DriveSpace resizes the drive specified by the *drive:* parameter. (You can abbreviate this switch to /res.)
drive:	Specifies the compressed drive that you want to resize. You must specify a drive when you use the /size switch.

If you enter DRVSPACE alone, DOS starts the DriveSpace program, in which you can use menu options to change the size of a compressed drive.

Sample

To resize your compressed drive C so that it's as large as possible, you enter

```
drvspace /size /reserve=0 c:
```

DRVSPACE (Uncompress)

Uncompresses a drive that was compressed by using DRVSPACE. In DOS 6.22+, DriveSpace replaces the utility that's known as DoubleSpace in Versions 6.0 and 6.20 (no disk compression utility is included with MS-DOS 6.21 and versions prior to 6.0).

This command is safe only in the hands of a programmer or some other totally DOSsed person. Stay clear unless they give you hazard pay.

DOSspeak

```
DRVSPACE [/uncompress] [drive:]
```

Variable or Option	Function
/uncompress	Tells DOS to uncompress the specified disk.
drive:	Specifies the letter of the compressed drive.

DRVSPACE (Unmount)

Breaks a connection between a compressed volume file (CVF) and a drive letter, making the CVF files temporarily unusable. In DOS 6.22+, DriveSpace replaces the utility that's known as DoubleSpace in Versions 6.0 and 6.20 (no disk compression utility is included with MS-DOS 6.21 and versions prior to 6.0).

DOSspeak

```
DRVSPACE [/unmount] [drive:]
```

Variable or Option	Function
/unmount	Unmounts the compressed drive specified by the *drive:* parameter. (You can abbreviate this switch to /u.)
drive:	Specifies the letter of the compressed drive to unmount. If you omit this parameter, DriveSpace unmounts the current drive.

If you enter DRVSPACE alone, DOS starts the DriveSpace program, in which you can use menu options to unmount a compressed drive.

Sample

To unmount compressed drive A, you enter

```
drvspace /unmount a:
```

EDIT

Starts the DOS Editor that you can use to edit text files, such as those weird AUTOEXEC.BAT and CONFIG.SYS files that application programs are always trying to get you to edit.

The EDIT command that ships with Windows 98 supports long filenames. Yeah! I still prefer Notepad.

DOSspeak

```
EDIT [[drive:][path]filename] [/b] [/g] [/h]
    [/nohi]
```

Variable or Option	Function
[drive:][path]filename	Specifies the drive, directory, and name of a new or existing file that you want to edit.
/b	Forces the Editor to appear in monochrome on a color monitor (use this switch to increase the screen contrast on a laptop that normally uses shades of gray to represent colors).
/g	Provides the fastest possible screen response when using the Editor with CGA graphics (the old standard Color/Graphics adapter).
/h	Displays the maximum number of lines possible on your monitor.
/nohi	Suppresses the display of high-intensity video while using the Editor. (Don't use this switch on laptops, because it routinely crashes them.)

Sample

Suppose that there's no way around it: Al in Finance is on vacation in Tahiti for the rest of the month, so you have to bite the bullet and edit the AUTOEXEC.BAT file on your computer *all by yourself!* To start the DOS Editor and load this file, you enter

```
edit c:\autoexec.bat
```

After (carefully) making and checking over your changes to this crucial file, press Alt+F, X and then press Y when asked whether you want to save your changes.

EDLIN

Starts that truly dreadful EDLIN Editor that you can use to edit text files (if absolutely nothing else is available and your boss refuses to upgrade to the latest version of DOS. However, if you get the boss to upgrade, *see* EDIT and forget the rest of this entry).

DOSspeak

EDLIN [*drive:*][*path*]*filename* [/b]

Variable or Option	Function
[*drive:*][*path*]*filename*	Specifies the drive, directory, and name of a new or existing file that you want to edit with EDLIN.
/b	Causes EDLIN to ignore all Ctrl+Z characters (those end-of-line thingies) in the file.

EXE2BIN

Converts an executable file (that is, a file with an EXE extension) to a binary-image format (that is, a file with a BIN extension) — and who said DOS commands were hard to understand?

This DOS command (as if you couldn't guess) is for advanced programmers, preferably those with Assembly language experience — all others need not apply!

DOSspeak

EXE2BIN [*drive1:*][*path1*]*input-file*
      [[*drive2:*][*path2*]*output-file*]

Variable or Option	Function
[*drive1:*][*path1*]*input-file*	Specifies the drive, path, and name of the executable file (with the EXE extension) to be converted to the binary format.
[*drive2:*][*path2*]*output-file*	Specifies the drive, path, and name of the binary format file to be created from the *input-file*. If no *output-file* is specified, DOS names it with the same filename as that of the *input-file* and adds a BIN extension to the main filename.

Sample

Suppose (for argument's sake, at least) that you've just finished creating your first executable file, called EXILEDOS.EXE, and now you want to convert it to a binary format. To do so, you enter

```
exe2bin exiledos
```

and DOS converts EXILEDOS.EXE to EXILEDOS.BIN.

EXIT

Returns control from a second copy of the command interpreter (started with the COMMAND command) to the parent command interpreter.

Also returns you to Windows from the DOS prompt.

See COMMAND for information on how to start the trouble that the EXIT command will get you out of.

DOSspeak

```
EXIT
```

Sample

Suppose that you're working away in Lotus 1-2-3. When you decide to save a file, instead of typing /fs as you normally do, you mess up and type /s. You find yourself facing a blank screen with the DOS prompt where 1-2-3 and your worksheet should be (/s is 1-2-3's way of starting a second DOS command interpreter). To get back home to your 1-2-3 worksheet, you type

```
exit
```

at the DOS prompt; then, press Enter to quit the second command interpreter and return immediately to 1-2-3 and your still unsaved worksheet.

EXPAND

Expands one or more compressed files (available in Versions 5+).

DOSspeak

```
EXPAND [drive:][path]filename
       [[drive1][path1]filename[...]] destination
```

Variable or Option	Function
[*drive:*][*path*]*filename*	Specifies the drive, path, and name of the file or files that you want to expand. Note that you can't use wildcards in the *filename* parameter. To expand multiple files, you must list all the filenames, separated by spaces.
destination	Specifies the new location and/or filename of the expanded file. If you are expanding multiple files, the *destination* parameter must consist solely of a *drive:* and/or *path* parameter without a *filename* parameter.

Sample

Al in Finance has given you a floppy disk with two compressed files called MEGAFILE.WK1 and MAMMOTH.DOC. To copy and expand these files in the \MYTURF directory on your hard disk, you put the floppy disk in drive A. At the C> prompt, you enter

```
expand a:megafile.wk1 a:mammoth.doc c:\myturf
```

FASTHELP

Displays a list of all DOS 6 commands with a brief explanation of each (available only in DOS 6 — not included in the Windows 98 version).

DOSspeak

```
FASTHELP [command]
```

where command is the DOS command that you want help on. If you enter FASTHELP without the *command* parameter, DOS displays an alphabetical list of all Version 6 commands.

Sample

You've forgotten how you use the MORE command to display just a screenful of info at a time. To get fast help on this command, you enter

```
fasthelp more
```

You can also get fast help by entering

```
more /?
```

at the DOS prompt.

FASTOPEN

Decreases the amount of time needed to open frequently used files and directories on the hard disk by storing their locations in a special part of memory called the *filename cache*. Not included in the Windows 98 version of DOS.

Note: Although FASTOPEN can boost performance in some limited situations, it's also true that this command requires a great deal of memory to hold the locations of the files in the filename cache. Be careful that you don't find yourself creating a state of affairs in which you not only don't get better performance but actually have trouble running some of your more memory-intensive applications.

You can't use FASTOPEN on a drive under the influence of the ASSIGN, JOIN, or SUBST command, nor can you use it on a network drive.

DOSspeak

`FASTOPEN drive:[[=]n] [drive:[[=]n] [...] [/x]`

Variable or Option	Function
drive:	Specifies the hard drive(s) whose files and directories you want FASTOPEN to remember. In versions prior to 5, you can specify up to four hard drives. In Versions 5+, you can specify up to 24 hard drives.
n	Specifies the maximum number of file locations that FASTOPEN retains in its filename cache (48 is the default on each *drive:*). The *n* parameter can be a number between 10 and 999. When specifying multiple drives, the total of all locations can't exceed 999.
	In Versions 4+, you can include a second number (between 1 and 999) in the *n* parameter. The second number specifies the number of buffers that can hold the location of fragmented parts of files on each drive (the so-called file-extent entries). When specifying these buffers, you need to enclose the *n* parameter in parentheses and enter its number after the file locations, separated by a comma — for example, (100,20), where 100 is the number of file locations and 20 is the number of file-extent entries.
/x	(Versions 4+) Specifies that FASTOPEN store the file locations in expanded memory (which must conform to the LIM 4.0 specification).

Remember: You can use FASTOPEN only once per work session. To change the FASTOPEN settings, you must reset your computer. Note that DOS uses about 48K of RAM memory for each file location that it stores. Each time you open a file, DOS adds the name and location to the filename cache. When the cache is full, DOS removes the last-accessed file from the list to make room for the new file.

Sample

Suppose that something possesses you to use FASTOPEN on your hard disk. To do this really strange thing, you enter

```
fastopen c:
```

FC

Compares two files or sets of files and reports back on any differences between them.

DOSspeak

```
FC [/a] [/c] [/l] [/lbn] [/n] [/t] [/w] [/nnnn]
    [drive1:][path1]filename1
    [drive2:][path2]filename2
```

or

```
FC [/b] [drive1:][path1]filename1
    [drive2:][path2]filename2
```

Variable or Option	Function
[drive1:][path1]filename1	Specifies the drive, path, and name of the first file or set of files you want to compare.
[drive2:][path2]filename2	Specifies the drive, path, and name of the second file or set of files you want to compare.
/a	Shortens the report by displaying only the first and last lines for each set of differences.
/b	Performs a binary comparison in which DOS compares the files byte by byte and reports the offset location of all differences. When using the /b switch, all other switches except the /nnnn switch are off limits.
/c	Ignores case differences when comparing text (ASCII) files — DOS treats the text as if it were entered in all uppercase letters.

Variable or Option	Function
/l	Forces DOS to perform a line-by-line comparison of the files as if they were ASCII files (the default, except when the file extension is EXE, COM, SYS, OBJ, LIB, or BIN).
/lb*n*	Sets the maximum number of consecutive mismatches in the difference report to the number of lines specified by the *n* parameter (the default is 100 lines).
/n	Displays line numbers when performing an ASCII comparison.
/t	Causes DOS to compare the tabs in the files literally; when the /t switch isn't used, DOS expands tabs to eight spaces.
/w	Causes DOS to ignore leading and trailing spaces and tabs in the files, and to compress consecutive tabs and spaces in a line down to a single space.
/*nnnn*	Specifies the number of consecutive lines (or bytes in a binary comparison) that must match after DOS finds a mismatch. If a number less than the number entered as the *nnnn* parameter is found, DOS includes the match in the difference report (the default is 2).

Sample

Suppose that while doing a directory listing of your \MYTURF directory, you find two word-processing files that you're pretty sure contain the same stuff even though they have different names (LETTER.DOC and EPISTLE.TXT). Do an ASCII file comparison to find out whether they're the same by entering

```
fc letter.doc epistle.txt
```

Next, you switch to your \123STUFF directory where you notice two worksheets (BIGBUCKS.WK1 and LOTLUCRE.WK1) that you think might be duplicates. To do a binary file comparison to find out, you enter

```
fc /b bigbucks.wk1 lotlucre.wk1
```

FIND

Searches for a string of characters in a file or set of files.

DOSspeak

```
FIND [/v] [/c] [/n] [/i] "string"
     [[drive:][path]filename[...]]
```

Variable or Option	Function
/v	Displays all lines that do NOT contain the string. If you use this switch with the /c switch, DOS reports the total number of lines that don't contain the *string*.
/c	Displays only the total number of lines that contain the string.
/n	Displays the line numbers along with the lines that contain the string.
/i	(Versions 5+) Ignores the case of the characters when searching for the string.
"string"	Specifies the string of characters to search for. The string parameter must be enclosed in a closed pair of quotation marks and is case sensitive unless you use the /i switch in the FIND command.
[*drive:*][*path*]*filename*	Specifies the drive, directory, and name of the file to be searched. To have DOS search multiple files, list each filename, separated by a space. If you omit this parameter, DOS searches your keyboard input until you press Ctrl+Z or F6 to terminate the input.

Sample

Suppose that you want to know how many lines in your work-for-hire contract called INDENTUR.DOC contain the phrase *grovel at my feet* (it's been one of those weeks!). To do so, you enter

```
find "grovel at my feet" indentur.doc /c
```

FORMAT

Prepares a new disk so that DOS can store files on it. Keep in mind, however, that FORMAT is lethal to disks that already contain files because it wipes their little data banks totally clean!

If you're using DOS 5 or later and (knock on wood) you reformat a floppy disk that has valuable data on it, you may be able to recover the files (or most of them, anyway) with the UNFORMAT command, provided that you use that command before you put any new files on this disk. In DOS 6.22+, DriveSpace replaces the utility that's known as DoubleSpace in Versions 6.0 and 6.20 (no disk compression utility is included with MS-DOS 6.21 and versions prior to 6.0). *Note:* FORMAT is not included with Windows 98.

DOSspeak

FORMAT *drive:* [/v[:*label*]] [/q] [/u] [/f:*size*] [/b]
    [/s] [c]

or

FORMAT *drive:* [/v[:*label*]] [/q] [/u] [/t:*tracks*
    /n:*sectors*] [/b] [/s] [c]

or

FORMAT *drive:* [/v[:*label*]] [/q] [/u] [/1] [/4] [/8]
    [/b] [/s] [c]

Variable or Option	Function
drive:	Specifies the letter of the drive that contains the disk you want formatted. Unless you really intend to wipe out all the data on your hard disk, you will want to restrict this *drive:* parameter to only A or B, the designation for your first and second floppy disk drives, respectively.
/v[:*label*]	In versions before 4, indicates that you want to assign a volume label to the disk (versions after 4 automatically prompt you to enter a volume label when you format the disk). In Versions 4+, you can avoid the label prompt by specifying a *label* parameter with the /v switch that contains the text of the volume label (up to 11 characters) following a colon.
/q	(Versions 5+) Performs a quick format of a previously formatted disk.
/u	(Versions 5+) Performs an unconditional format that destroys all previous data on the disk — data that cannot later be restored with the UNFORMAT command. (This type of formatting is what versions of DOS before 5.0 perform.)
/f:*size*	(Versions 4+) Specifies the size of the disk to format. *Size* parameters can include 160 for a 160K disk, 180 for 180K, 320 for 320K, 360 for 360K, 720 for 720K, 1.2 for 1.2MB, 1.44 for 1.44MB, and 2.88 (Versions 5+) for 2.88MB. Don't use this switch with the /1, /8, /t, or /n switch.
/b	Formats the disk to use only 8 sectors per track (even when formatting a disk with 9 or 15 sectors) and leaves space for the DOS system files (without copying them on the disk — use SYS to do this part). You can't use this switch with the /t or /s switch.

(continued)

Variable or Option	Function
/s	Copies the system files to the formatted disk so that you can boot from that disk.
/c	Instructs the FORMAT command to retest bad clusters. (This was the default in previous versions of DOS.)
/t:tracks	(Version 3.3 only) Specifies the number of tracks on the formatted disk.
/n:sectors	(Version 3.3 only) Specifies the number of sectors per track on the formatted disk.
/1	Formats only one side of a floppy disk.
/4	(Versions 3.2+) Formats a double-density (360K) disk in a high-density (1.2MB) drive.
/8	Formats 8 sectors per track on 5¼-inch floppy disks rather than the normal 9 for double-sided or 15 for high-density disks. You can't use this switch with the /t or /v switch.

Sample

Your department has run out of new high-density (1.2MB) 5¼-inch floppy disks, and you need to copy some files for Al in Finance. You decide to trash an old high-density disk that you find in the Boss's office. To reformat this disk, you enter

```
format a:
```

Later that day, Sue comes over with a new double-density 5¼-inch disk and asks you to format it for her (she can't do it because Cindy's doing payroll on her machine). Because you know Sue's computer has only a double-sided floppy drive, you enter the following command to format her disk on your high-density floppy drive:

```
format a: /4
```

Note that you can also accomplish this task by entering

```
format a: /f:360
```

GRAFTABL

Enables your computer to display special graphics characters on-screen when you have a color/graphics adapter and the computer is in graphics mode.

DOSspeak

GRAFTABL [*xxx* | /status]

Variable or Option	Function
xxx	Specifies the number of the code page whose character set is to be used. Code page numbers include 437 for American (English), 850 for Multilingual, 860 for Portuguese, 863 for French-Canadian, and 865 for Nordic.
/status	Displays the number of the active code page (this can be abbreviated to /sta).

If you enter GRAFTABL with no parameters, DOS lists the number of the previous code page.

Sample

Cousin Olaf wants to use your computer again, this time to compose an old Norse hymn to Odin with lots of strange-looking runic characters in it. You obviously need to switch him over to the Nordic code page, so you enter

```
graftabl 865
```

After entering this command, you check to see whether your computer is ready for rune(s) by entering

```
graftabl /sta
```

GRAPHICS

Enables you to print a screen containing graphics characters on an IBM-compatible printer with the Print Screen key (a.k.a. Shift+PrintScrn). Not included in the Windows 98 version of DOS.

DOSspeak

GRAPHICS [*type*] [[*drive:*[*path*]*filename*] [/r] [/b]
[/lcd] [/printbox:*id*]

Variable or Option	Function
type	Specifies the type of printer (see following table).
[*drive:*[*path*]*filename*]	(Versions 4+) Specifies the name of the drive, the path, and the printer profile file. If you omit this parameter, DOS uses the GRAPHICS.PRO file.

(continued)

Variable or Option	Function
/r	Reverses the foreground and background in the printout so that it resembles the screen more closely (with white characters on a black background).
/b	Prints the background in color when the *type* parameter is color4 or color8 (see the following table).
/lcd	Prints the image from the Liquid Crystal Display (LCD) of an IBM PC Convertible.
/printbox:*id*	(Versions 4+) Specifies the size of the printbox. *id* is the first parameter following the Printbox Statement in your printer profile. When using the GRAPHICS.PRO file for your printer information, the *id* parameter is either std or lcd.

The *type* parameter can be any of the following:

Type	Printer
color1	IBM PC Color Printer with a black ribbon or the black band of a color ribbon
color4	IBM PC Color Printer with a red-green-blue-black color ribbon
color8	IBM PC Color Printer with a cyan-magenta-yellow-black color ribbon
compact	(Version 3.3 only) IBM PC Compact Printer
graphics	IBM Personal Graphics Printer, Proprinter, or Quietwriter
graphicswide	(Versions 4+) IBM Personal Graphics Printer, Proprinter, or Quietwriter with wide carriage
thermal	IBM PC Convertible Thermal Printer
hpdefault	(Versions 5+) Any Hewlett-Packard PCL printer
deskjet	(Versions 5+) HP Deskjet
laserjet	(Versions 5+) HP Laserjet
laserjetii	(Versions 5+) HP Laserjet Series II
paintjet	(Versions 5+) HP Paintjet
quietjet	(Versions 5+) HP Quietjet
quietjetplus	(Versions 5+) HP Quietjet Plus
ruggedwriter	(Versions 5+) HP Rugged Writer
ruggedwriterwide	(Versions 5+) HP Rugged Writer with wide carriage
thinkjet	(Versions 5+) HP Thinkjet

If you use GRAPHICS with no no parameters, DOS will load the command, using the graphics *type* parameter (as described in the preceding table).

Sample

You need to print a screen that contains lines and boxes to include in a report. Your printer is an HP Laserjet Series II. Before pressing the Print Screen key, you enter

```
graphics laserjetii
```

HELP

In Versions 6.0 to 6.22, starts a menu-driven utility that gives you help information on any DOS command. In earlier versions, displays an alphabetical list of all DOS and batch commands or a short description of a particular command (including the DOSspeak line and a listing of the parameters).

DOSspeak

```
HELP [command]
```

where *command* is the name of the DOS command that you want help information on. To get help on a command right before you execute it (which might be a little risky), type the command followed by the /? switch.

Sample

Suppose that Sue has borrowed your copy of *DOS For Dummies Quick Reference,* 3rd Edition. You can't look up the DOSspeak for the FORMAT command, and you've forgotten the switch for formatting a double-sided disk in your high-density drive. To get help on this command, you enter

```
help format
```

After DOS spits out the FORMAT DOSspeak on-screen, you decide that you really need a printout of this stuff. To send the gobbledygook on FORMAT to your printer rather than your screen, this time you enter

```
help format >prn
```

INTERLNK

Connects two computers via their parallel or serial ports so that they can share information and resources such as a printer (available only in DOS 6 — not included in the Windows 98 version of DOS).

In order to use the INTERLNK command, the INTERLNK.EXE device driver must be installed (*see* DEVICE in Part V) and the Interlnk server must be running (*see* INTERSVR).

This command is safe only in the hands of a programmer or some other totally DOSsed person. Stay clear unless they give you hazard pay.

DOSspeak

```
INTERLNK [client[:]=[server][:]]
```

Variable or Option	Function
client	Specifies the letter of the client drive that is to be redirected to a drive on the Interlnk server. The drive letter you give for the *client* parameter must be one that was redirected when you started Interlnk (see INTERSVR).
server	Specifies the letter of the drive on the Interlnk server that will be redirected. This drive must be one of those listed on the This Computer (Server) column of the Interlnk server screen. If you omit the *server* parameter, Interlnk no longer redirects the client drive specified by the *client* parameter.

If you enter INTERLNK with no parameters, DOS displays the current status of the interlinked drives.

Sample

Suppose that the Interlnk server is running and drive D is one of the server drives. To redirect client drive F to drive D on the server, you enter

```
interlnk f=d
```

Later, to cancel the redirection of client drive F, you enter

```
interlnk f=
```

INTERSVR

Starts the Interlnk server and specifies how the server's drives are to be redirected and which ports are used to connect to the client (available only in DOS 6 — not included in the Windows 98 version of DOS).

Before you can use the INTERSVR command, the INTERLNK.EXE device driver must be installed (*see* DEVICE in Part V). Also, you can't use the INTERSVR command to redirect network drives or drives like CD-ROM drives that use a redirection interface, nor can you use INTERSVR with the CHKDSK, DEFRAG, DISKCOMP, DISKCOPY, FDISK, FORMAT, MIRROR, SYS, UNDELETE, or UNFORMAT command.

This command is safe only in the hands of a programmer or some other totally DOSsed person. Stay clear unless they give you hazard pay.

DOSspeak

To start the Interlnk server:

```
INTERSVR [drive:[...]] [/x=drive:[...]] [/lpt:[n |
    address]] [/com:[n |address]] [/baud:rate] [/b]
    [/v]
```

To copy the Interlnk files from one computer to another:

```
INTERSVR [/rcopy]
```

Variable or Option	Function
drive:	Specifies the letter(s) of the server drive(s) to be redirected to client drives. If you omit the *drive:* parameter, all server drives are redirected. To specify multiple server drives, separate drive letters with a space.
/x=*drive*	Specifies the letter(s) of the server drive(s) not to be redirected to a client drive(s). Keep in mind that, by default, all drives are redirected.
/lpt:[n	*address*]	Specifies a parallel port to use. You can specify which port to use with either an *n* parameter that specifies the number of the LPT port or an *address* parameter that specifies the port's address. If you omit the *n* or *address* parameter, Interlnk uses the first parallel port that it finds.
/com: [n	*address*]	Specifies a serial port to use. You can specify which port to use with either an *n* parameter that specifies the number of the COM port or an *address* parameter that specifies the port's address. If you omit the *n* or *address* parameter, Interlnk uses the first serial port that it finds.
/baud:*rate*	Specifies the baud rate. The *rate* parameter can be any of the following: 9600, 19200, 38400, 57600, or 115200 (the default).
/b	Displays the Interlnk server screen in black and white.

(continued)

Variable or Option	Function
/v	Prevents conflicts with a computer's timer when using a serial connection between computers; one stops running when you use Interlnk to access a drive or printer port.
/rcopy	Copies the Interlnk files from one computer to another when they are connected with a 7-wire, null-modem serial cable (what else would you use?) and the MODE command is available on the computer where you're installing Interlnk.

If you enter INTERSVR with no parameters, DOS starts the Interlnk server and displays the Interlnk server screen, using the default display.

Sample

To start the Interlnk server and specify that drives C and A on the server be redirected to the client as drives D and E, respectively, you enter

```
intersvr c: a:
```

JOIN

Joins a disk drive to a directory on another drive so that the entire directory structure of the disk drive *appears* as a subdirectory on the other drive and *the first drive letter is no longer available.*

Stay away from this command unless you're absolutely sure that you know what you're doing. Also, even if you do know what you're doing, avoid using this command on any drive under the influence of the ASSIGN or SUBST command.

DOSspeak

```
JOIN [drive1: [drive2:]path]
```

or

```
JOIN drive1: /d
```

Variable or Option	Function
drive1:	Specifies the drive whose entire directory will appear as a directory on *drive2.*
drive2:	Specifies the drive to which drive1 is to be joined.

Variable or Option	Function
path	Specifies the directory on drive2 where drive1 will appear. This directory must be empty and must not be the drive2 root directory.
/d	Cancels the join between drives (as does resetting the computer).

If you enter JOIN with no parameters, DOS lists the joins in effect (if none are in effect, nothing is just what DOS displays).

Sample

Suppose that you want to join the disk in drive A to a new (empty) subdirectory called \ALIAS_A that you've created on drive C. To do this crazy thing, you enter

```
join a: c:\alias_a
```

Okay, you've had your fun doing directory listings of C:\ALIAS_A and getting a list of the files on drive A. Now, you're ready to sever the connection before you get into some real trouble. To do so, you enter

```
join a: /d
```

KEYB

Changes the keyboard layout from the U.S. default to one for a particular foreign language.

TIP

In DOS versions prior to 3.3, you can load a new keyboard layout with the KEYB command only once per work session. In later versions, you can use the command as often as necessary to switch to different layouts. In all versions, you can switch back to the default (U.S.) keyboard at any time by pressing Ctrl+Alt+F1; then, return to the keyboard layout you loaded with KEYB by pressing Ctrl+Alt+F2.

DOSspeak

```
KEYB [xx[,[yyy][,[drive:][path]filename]]] [/e]
    [/id:nnn]
```

Variable or Option	Function
xx	Specifies a two-letter keyboard code (see following tables).
yyy	Specifies the code page for the character set (see the second table following).
[drive:][path]filename	Specifies the drive, directory, and name of the file with the keyboard definition file KEYBOARD.SYS. If you omit this parameter, DOS looks for this file in the directories in the search path (**see** PATH).
/e	(Versions 5+) Specifies that an enhanced keyboard is installed (one of those babies with 101 or 102 keys that you're dying to get your hands on).
/id:nnn	(Versions 4+) Specifies the keyboard ID (see second table following) for countries with more than one enhanced keyboard (such as France, Italy, and the UK).

In DOS versions prior to 3.3, the KEYB command uses only the two-letter keyboard codes as shown in the following table. When using one of these codes as the *xx* parameter, the parameter must follow the keyboard command with no spaces — for example, keybit to switch to the Italian keyboard layout.

Two-Letter Keyboard Code	Country
uk	United Kingdom
gr	Germany
fr	France
it	Italy
sp	Spain

In DOS Versions 3.3+, you specify both the keyboard code as the *xx* parameter and a code page number as the *yyy* parameter. (Note, however, that the code page numbers are different in Versions 3.3 and 4+.) In Versions 4+, you can also specify a keyboard ID as the *nnn* parameter when a country supports more than one enhanced keyboard. The following table shows all these codes:

Keyboard Code	Code Page Number: V3.3 | V4+	Keyboard ID	Keyboard Layout
us	001 | 437	103	USA (the default)
cf	002 | 863	058	Canada (French)
fr	033 | 437	189 or 120	France

Keyboard Code	Code Page Number: V3.3 | V4+	Keyboard ID	Keyboard Layout
gr	049 | 437	129	Germany
it	039 | 437	141 or 142	Italy
sp	034 | 437	172	Spain
uk	044 | 437	166 or 168	United Kingdom
po	351 | 860	163	Portugal
sg	041 | 437	000	Switzerland (German)
sf	041 | 437	150	Switzerland (French)
dk	045 | 865	159	Denmark
be	032 | 437	120	Belgium
nl	031 | 437	143	Netherlands
no	047 | 865	155	Norway
la	003 | 437	171	Latin America
sv	046 | 437	153	Sweden
sv	046 | 437	153	Finland

When you enter KEYB with no parameters, DOS displays the current keyboard code page.

Sample

Cousin Olaf is using your computer again, this time to compose a Norse heroic saga. But he's complaining about what he calls "this fancy-pants U. S. of A. keyboard," and he wants the keyboard to act "like the one we use in old country." To switch him over to the Nordic keyboard layout and make him happy, you enter

```
keyb no,865
```

LABEL

Enables you to add, modify, or delete a volume label from a formatted floppy or hard disk.

You can't use the LABEL command with a drive under the influence of our old friends ASSIGN, JOIN, or SUBST.

DOSspeak

```
LABEL [drive:][label]
```

Variable or Option	Function
drive:	Specifies the letter of the drive containing the disk whose volume label you want to adjust. If you don't specify a *drive:* parameter, DOS assumes that you want to work with the disk in the current drive.
label	Specifies the volume label (up to 11 characters) that you want assigned to the disk specified by the *drive:* parameter. If you don't specify a *label* parameter, DOS displays the current label and prompts you to enter a new one. To delete the label, just press Enter and then press Y to the Delete current volume label (Y/N)? prompt.

Sample

Suppose that you didn't assign a label to your floppy disk when you formatted it, but now that you've backed up a number of important spreadsheet files, you want to label the disk SERIOUS_123. To do so, put the floppy disk in drive A and then enter

```
label a: serious_123
```

LH or LOADHIGH

Loads a terminate-and-stay-resident (TSR) program into upper (reserved) memory area on an Intel 386- or 486-based computer. (Available in Versions 5+ only.)

You don't have to abbreviate this command to LH — if you're really into typing, you can enter LOADHIGH instead.

DOSspeak

LH [*drive:*][*path*]*filename* [*parameters*]

or

LH [/l:*region1*[,*minsize1*][;*region2*[,*minsize2*]]
    [/s]]=[*drive:*][*path*]**filename** [*dd-parameters*]

Variable or Option	Function
[*drive:*][*path*]*filename*	Specifies the drive, path, and name of the TSR program command file that you want to load into reserved memory.
parameters	Specifies any command line parameters that the program requires to load.

Variable or Option	Function
/l:*region1*[,*minsize1*] [;*region2*[,*minsize2*]]	Specifies one or more regions of memory into which the device driver is to be loaded. To ensure that a driver won't be loaded into a region that's too small for it, you can also specify the *minsize* parameter for the particular *region* parameter that you specify.
/s	Normally used by the MemMaker program to shrink the UMB (upper memory block) to its minimum size while the device drive is loading. Don't use this /s switch unless you're certain that shrinking the UMB won't interfere with loading the device driver. You can use the /s switch only with the /l switch and only when you've specified both a *region* and a *minsize* parameter.

Before you can use the LH (LOADHIGH) command, your CONFIG.SYS (System Configuration) file must first have loaded the HIMEM.SYS device driver plus an expanded memory manager, such as the EMM386.EXE device driver. *See* DEVICE in Part V for more information.

Sample

Today, you're using the 486 computer that your boss (who's away on business in Europe) uses. You decide that you want to load the DOSKEY utility to make it easier to recall and edit your DOS commands as you work. To load the DOSKEY utility in the reserved memory of the boss's 486, you enter

```
lh doskey
```

LOADFIX

Loads a program above the first 64K of conventional memory (Versions 5+ only). Use the LOADFIX command only after you've received a Packed file corrupt error message when trying to run an older program under DOS 5+.

Most application programs have no need for LOADFIX unless they are truly ancient (in which case, maybe you should upgrade them).

DOSspeak

```
LOADFIX [drive:][path]filename
```

where [*drive:*][*path*]*filename* specifies the drive, path, and name of the program file that runs the program you want to load with LOADFIX.

MD or MKDIR

Creates a new directory on your disk.

You don't have to abbreviate this command to MD — DOS knows it as MKDIR as well.

DOSspeak

`MD [drive:][path]name`

Variable or Option	Function
drive:	Specifies the drive on whose disk the new directory is to be created.
path	Specifies the existing directory in which the new directory will be created (thus making the new directory one of the subdirectories of the existing directory).
name	Specifies the name of the new directory. This directory *name* can be no more than eight characters long with a three-character extension (and no spaces) — just like a filename. If you specify a *path* parameter, you must precede the *name* parameter with a \ (backslash). If the name already exists in the location specified by the *drive:* and *path* parameters, DOS gives you the error message Unable to create directory.

Sample

Suppose that you need to create a subdirectory of your \MYTURF directory to store all the legal documents you work with (so you'll call it LEGSTUFF). To create this new directory when your \MYTURF directory is current, you enter

`md legstuff`

Now you remember that you also need to create a new directory for your assistant to keep files separate from yours. You want this directory to be on the same level as your \MYTURF directory (right below the root on drive C), and you decide to call it ASTJUNK. To create this directory, you enter

`md \astjunk`

MEM

Displays the amount of free and used memory in your computer (available in Versions 4+).

If you're using a version of DOS prior to 4.0, you can use the CHKDSK command to see how much memory your computer has.

DOSspeak

In versions prior to DOS 6:

`MEM [/program | /debug | /classify]`

In Version 6:

`MEM [/classify | debug | /free | /module programname] [/page]`

Variable or Option	Function
/program	Displays the status of the programs currently loaded into memory. In Versions 5+, you can abbreviate this switch to /p.
/debug	Displays the status of the programs and system device drivers currently loaded into memory. In Versions 5+, you can abbreviate this switch to /d.
/classify	(Versions 5+) Classifies programs by their memory usage. Displays the size of the programs and gives you a summary of memory usage. You can abbreviate this switch to /c.
/free	Lists the free areas of conventional and upper memory. You can use this switch with /page but not with the other switches; you can abbreviate it to /f.
/module *programname*	Shows how a program name is currently using memory; you must specify the *programname* parameter with the /module switch. You can use this switch with /page but not with the other switches; you can abbreviate it to /m.
/page	Pauses after each screenful of information.

Sample

Suppose that you're working at the boss's 486 machine, and you suddenly become curious about just how much raw RAM this baby packs. To display the amount of used and free memory with the program classified by memory usage, you enter

`mem /c`

MEMMAKER

Starts the MemMaker program, which optimizes a 386 or 486 computer's memory by moving device drivers and terminate-and-stay-resident (TSR) programs to upper memory (available only in DOS 6 — not included in the Windows 98 version).

Don't use the MEMMAKER command while you are running Microsoft Windows.

DOSspeak

MEMMAKER [/b] [/batch] [/session] [/swap:*drive*]
    [/t] [/undo] [/w:*size1,size2*]

Variable or Option	Function
/b	Displays MemMaker in black and white. Use this switch when the program isn't displayed correctly on a monochrome monitor.
/batch	Runs MemMaker in batch (unattended) mode where the program supplies the default responses to each prompt. If an error occurs, MemMaker restores your previous AUTOEXEC.BAT and CONFIG.SYS files and, if necessary, Windows SYSTEM.INI files. After the batch process is complete, you can review the session in a file called MEMMAKER.STS that you can open with the DOS Editor (*see* EDIT).
/session	This switch is used only by MemMaker when optimizing your computer's memory.
/swap:*drive*	Specifies that the drive letter for the startup disk has changed since booting your computer (some disk compression utilities change startup drive letters when they swap compressed and uncompressed files). Specify the modified drive letter as the /swap *drive* parameter. Don't use this switch with the Stacker 2.0, SuperStor, or Microsoft DoubleSpace — *see* DBLSPACE (Compress) — compression utilities.
/t	Disables the detection of IBM Token-Ring networks so that you can use MemMaker on such a network.
/undo	Undoes the most recent changes to your AUTOEXEC.BAT, CONFIG.SYS and, if affected, Windows SYSTEM.INI files. Then you can return to your previous memory configuration if you're not satisfied with the job MemMaker did.
/w:*size1,size2*	Specifies how much upper memory space to reserve for Windows translation buffers. The *size1* parameter specifies how much memory to reserve for the first translation buffer area; the *size2* parameter specifies how much to reserve for the second area (the default is no upper memory for the Windows translation buffers).

If you enter MEMMAKER with no parameters, DOS starts the MemMaker program, which prompts you for the drivers and memory-resident programs to load into upper memory.

Sample

To run the MemMaker program on your boss's 486 computer in batch mode, you enter

```
memmaker /batch
```

Later, your boss indicates a preference for the computer before you optimized the memory. To restore the previous memory configuration, you enter

```
memmaker /undo
```

MIRROR

Records disk information about a specified drive that the UNFORMAT command can later use to help recover its files — that's if you just happen to reformat the disk (oops!) by mistake. (Available in Version 5 only.)

Even if you don't use the MIRROR command to record information about your disk, it may still be possible to recover your files (at least some of them) with the UNFORMAT command — *see* UNFORMAT for more information.

Don't use the MIRROR command on a drive under the influence of the JOIN or SUBST command.

DOSspeak

```
MIRROR [drive:[...]] [/1] [/tdrive[-entries][...]]
```

or

```
MIRROR [/u]
```

or

```
MIRROR [/partn]
```

Variable or Option	Function
drive:	Specifies the drive whose file and directory information you want to save. To specify more than one drive, separate the *drive:* parameters by a space. If you omit the *drive:* parameter, DOS uses the current drive.

(continued)

Variable or Option	Function
/1	Saves only the latest disk information in the MIRROR.FIL file in the root directory specified by the *drive:* parameter (does not save a backup called MIRROR.BAK).
/t*drive*	Loads the deletion-tracking program for the *drive:* specified after the /t switch. This program saves information each time you delete a file in the specified *drive:* in a special file called PCTRACKR.DEL, which is located in the root directory of the *drive:*.
-*entries*	Specifies the number of entries that the deletion-tracking program will save. Default values for the -*entries* parameter vary according to the size of the disk specified by the *drive:* parameter (see the following table).
/u	Unloads the deletion-tracking program.
/partn	Saves hard disk partition information in a file named PARTNSAV.FIL to a floppy disk.

As you can see from the following table, not only does the default number of entries saved by the deletion-tracking program vary according to the type of disk specified by the t/*drive* parameter, but so does the resulting size of the PCTRACKR.DEL file (yeoww!).

Type of Disk	Default Number of Entries	Size of the PCTRACKR.DEL File
360K	25	5K
720K	50	9K
1.2MB	75	14K
1.44MB	75	15K
20MB	101	18K
32MB	202	36K
over 32MB	303	55K

Sample

To record disk information about your hard disk (drive C) and load the deletion-tracking program, you enter

```
mirror /tc
```

MODE (Codepage)

Prepares and selects a code page (that is, a foreign character set) for a particular device.

When using the MODE command to prepare, select, or refresh a code page or get status information on the code page for a device, you can abbreviate the *codepage* parameter to *cp*. Also, when preparing a code page, you can abbreviate the *prepare* parameter to *prep*.

This command is safe only in the hands of a programmer or some other totally DOSsed person. Stay clear unless they give you hazard pay.

DOSspeak

To prepare the code page for use with a particular device:

MODE *device* codepage prepare=((*yyy*[...])
    [*drive:*][*path*]*filename*)

To select the code page and make it active for a particular device:

MODE *device* codepage select=*yyy*

To restore a previously selected code page to a particular device:

MODE *device* codepage refresh

To display information on the current code page status for a particular device:

MODE *device* codepage [/status]

Variable or Option	*Function*
device	Specifies the device that uses the code page. The *device* parameter can be CON (your console [monitor]), PRN (printer), LPT1 (printer on first parallel port), LPT2 (printer on second parallel port), or LPT3 (printer on third parallel port).
yyy	Specifies the number of the code page to be used with the device. The *yyy* parameter can be 437 for American (English), 850 for Multilingual, 860 for Portuguese, 863 for French-Canadian, or 865 for Nordic.
[*drive:*][*path*]*filename*	Specifies the drive, path, and name of the file with the code page information. When you omit the *drive:* and *path* parameters, DOS assumes that the file is located in the directories included in your path (**see** PATH).

(continued)

Variable or Option	Function
	In Version 3.3, the *filename* parameter can be EGA.CPI (for an EGA or VGA graphics adapter), LCD.CPI (for the IBM PC Convertible Liquid Crystal Display), 4201.CPI (for the IBM 4201 Proprinter family), 4208.CPI (for the IBM Proprinter X24 and XL24), or 5202.CPI (for the IBM Quietwriter III). Later versions of DOS can include other files (check your documentation for specifics). When entering the *filename* parameter, you can omit the CPI extension because it is assumed.
/status	(Versions 4+) This parameter is completely superfluous. If you feel that you just have to use it, you can abbreviate it to /sta rather than type the whole /status thing out.

Sample

Cousin Olaf wants to print his old Norse hymn to Odin on your printer. To get all the strange runic characters, you need to prepare code page 850 for your printer:

```
mode prn codepage prepare=(850) c:\dos\5202.cpi
```

After preparing the code page, you select it for your printer as follows:

```
mode prn codepage select=850
```

To make sure that your printer is now set up for Cousin Olaf, you then enter

```
mode prn codepage
```

MODE (Configure Printer)

Specifies the number of columns and lines for a printer connected to one of your parallel ports.

DOSspeak

```
MODE LPTn[:][c][,[l][,p]]
```

or (in Versions 4+)

```
MODE LPTn[:] [cols=c] [lines=l] [retry=r]
```

Variable or Option	Function
LPT*n*	Specifies the number of the parallel port (1, 2, or 3) to which your printer is attached. (*LPT* stands for *line printer*.)
c	Specifies the number of columns (and characters) to print per line. The *c* parameter can be 80 or 132 (with 80 as the default).
l	Specifies the number of lines to print per inch. The *l* parameter can be 6 or 8 (with 6 as the default).
p	(Versions 3.3 and earlier) Causes DOS to continuously retry to send the output when the printer is not ready (equivalent to retry=b in later versions — see next option).
r	(Versions 4+) Specifies the retry action that DOS should take when the printer is busy. The r parameter can be e (for return error), b (for return busy), *r* (for return ready), or none (to take no action).

Sample

Today, you're working at Cindy's computer, and she has a wide-carriage printer. You just tried printing a file from DOS, and you notice that the printout uses only the first 80 columns. Before you reprint the file, set the mode for Cindy's printer to 132 columns to take full advantage of the wide carriage and tell DOS to resend the print info if the printer is not ready (like when you forget to put the printer back online) by entering

```
mode lpt1 cols=132 retry=b
```

Unfortunately, when you press Enter, DOS gives you a nasty error message because Cindy's machine still uses Version 3.3 (when is she going to get with it?). To get her older version of DOS to listen to you, you rephrase the MODE command to

```
mode lpt1:132,,p
```

The extra comma indicates where you would put the number of lines per inch if you were changing this parameter — it must be there in Version 3.3 when you want to use the *p* (retry busy) parameter.

MODE (Configure Serial Port)

Specifies the parameters for a serial (communications) port that define the speed and how the data are transmitted.

If you're specifying a printer for your COM port, in addition to setting up the port settings with the MODE command, you also need to redirect the printer — *see* MODE (Redirect Parallel Printer) for details.

DOSspeak

MODE COM*m*[:]*b*[[,*p*[,*d*][,*s*[,*p*]]]]

or (in Versions 4+)

MODE COM*m*[:] [baud=*b*] [parity=*p*] [data=*d*] [stop=*s*] [retry=*r*]

Variable or Option	Function
COM*m*	Specifies the number of the serial (communications) port (1, 2, 3, or 4) to which the device is attached (the *COM* in COM1, COM2, and so on stands for *communications* because these ports are often used to connect devices, such as a modem, to your computer).
b	Specifies the baud rate (that is, the bits per second). The *b* parameter can be 110, 150, 300, 600, 1200, 2400, 4800, 9600, or 19200. You must specify a baud rate because there is no default.
p	Specifies the parity (error checking). The *p* parameter can be n (for none), o (for odd), or e (for even); also m (for mark) or s (for space) in Versions 4+. The default is e (for even).
d	Specifies the number of data bits. The *d* parameter can be 7 or 8; also 5 or 6 in Versions 4+. The default is 7 data bits.
s	Specifies the number of stop bits. The *s* parameter can be 1 or 2; also 1.5 in Versions 4+. If the *b* parameter is 110, *s* is 2 by default. Otherwise, the default is 1.
p	(Versions 3.3 and earlier) Causes DOS to continuously retry sending the output when the serial port is not ready (equivalent to retry=b in later versions — see the following).
r	(Versions 4+) Specifies the retry action that DOS should take when the serial port is busy. The *r* parameter can be e (for return error — the default), b (for return busy), r (for return ready), or none (to take no action).

Sample

When Mr. Peters retired, Sue inherited his old Diablo serial printer. She wants you (of all people) to help her configure DOS so that she can print with the fossil printer. You finally decipher from her printer manual that the baud rate should be set to 2400, the parity to None, data bits to 8, and stop bits to 1. To set up her first serial port for this printer, you enter

```
mode com1 baud=2400 parity=n data=8 stop=1
```

Unfortunately, when you press Enter, DOS gives you a nasty error message because Sue is still using Version 3.3 on her old klunker. To get this version of DOS to listen to you, you have to reenter the MODE command as

```
mode com1:2400,n,8,1
```

MODE (Device Status)

Displays current status information on a particular device on your system (Versions 4+).

DOSspeak

```
MODE [device] [/status]
```

Variable or Option	Function
device	Specifies the device for which you want the status information. The *device* parameter can be CON (your console [monitor]), PRN (printer), LPT1 (printer on first parallel port), LPT2 (printer on second parallel port), LPT3 (printer on third parallel port), COM1 (first serial port), COM2 (second serial port), COM3 (third serial port), or COM4 (fourth serial port).
/status	This parameter is not required unless you are requesting the status of a redirected parallel printer — *see* MODE (Redirect Parallel Printer). You can abbreviate this parameter to /sta.

If you enter MODE with no parameters, DOS gives you information on all the devices that are installed in your system.

Sample

To check the status of your first parallel port, you enter

```
mode lpt1
```

To check the status of this parallel port after you redirect it to your first serial port, you enter

```
mode lpt1 /sta
```

MODE (Display)

Selects the display and controls how the information is displayed.

DOSspeak

To select the display:

```
MODE [display-adapter][,n]
```

or

```
MODE CON[:] [cols=c] [lines=n]
```

To select a display and shift the image with CGA graphics:

```
MODE [display-adapter][,shift[,t]]
```

Variable or Option	Function
CON[:]	Indicates the display monitor.
display-adapter	Specifies the type of display. The *display-adapter* parameter can be mono (for monochrome adapter, 80 columns), 40 (for color/graphics adapter, 40 columns), 80 (for color/graphics adapter, 80 columns), bw40 (for color/graphics adapter, 40 columns with color disabled), bw80 (for color/graphics adapter, 80 columns with color disabled), co40 (for color/graphics adapter, 40 columns with color enabled), and co80 (for color/graphics adapter, 80 columns with color enabled).
n	(Versions 4+) Specifies the number of lines on the display. The *n* parameter varies according to the adapter and its settings. Typical values include 25, 43, and 50 (check your monitor documentation for permissible values).
c	(Versions 4+) Specifies the number of columns (that is, characters) that appear on each line on the display. The *c* parameter can be 40 or 80.

Variable or Option	Function
shift	Specifies whether to shift the screen display to the left (l) or right (r) when adjusting a display connected to a CGA adapter (this command does not work with EGA or VGA color/graphics adapters). When you specify r as the shift parameter, DOS shifts the display two columns to the right on an 80-column display or one column to the right on a 40-column display. When you specify l as this parameter, DOS adjusts the display the same amount but in the opposite (left) direction.
t	Causes DOS to display a test pattern that you can shift to the left or right until the display is aligned properly on your monitor.

Sample

To display 43 lines on your 16-inch color monitor attached to an EGA graphics card, you enter

```
mode con lines=43
```

MODE (Keyboard Typematic Rate)

Controls the rate at which the keys on your keyboard repeat (the so-called *typematic* effect) and the initial delay before the typematic effect kicks in.

DOSspeak

```
MODE CON[:] [rate=r delay=d]
```

Variable or Option	Function
CON[:]	Indicates the display monitor.
r	Specifies the rate at which a key repeats. The r parameter can be between 2 and 32, representing characters per second.
d	Specifies the initial delay before the key repeats. The d parameter can be 1 (for $1/4$ second), 2 (for $1/2$ second), 3 (for $3/4$ second), or 4 (for a full second).

Sample

To reduce the typematic interval to 15 (20 is the default) and increase the initial delay to $1/2$ second (from the $1/4$ default), you enter

```
mode con rate=15 delay=2
```

MODE *(Redirect Parallel Printer)*

Redirects the output from a parallel port to a printer connected to a serial (communications) port after you use the MODE command to configure the serial port — *see* MODE (Configure Serial Port).

DOSspeak

MODE LPT*n*[:]=COM*m*[:]

Variable or Option	Function
LPT*n*[:]	Specifies the number of the parallel port whose output is to be redirected. The *n* parameter can be 1, 2, or 3.
COM*m*[:]	Specifies the number of the serial port to which the output is redirected. The *m* parameter can be 1, 2, 3, or 4.

Sample

After you finish configuring Sue's COM1 serial port for her new, hand-me-down Diablo serial printer, you redirect the printer output to this port by entering

```
mode lpt1=com1
```

MORE

Instructs DOS to display text one screenful at time rather than in one big scrolling blur.

DOSspeak

MORE < [*drive:*][*path*]*filename*

or

command | MORE

Remember: When using the MORE command to control the display of a text file, you can either redirect input from the disk file, for example

```
more < read.me
```

or "pipe" the output of the TYPE command to the MORE command, for example

```
type read.me | more
```

The vertical bar (the shifted \ key) is called the *pipe character,* and it sends the result of one DOS command to another.

Sample

You've just gotten a new program. Before you install it, the documentation tells you to read a file called SETUP.TXT. When you use the TYPE command to display this file, pages and pages of stuff fly by in one big blur. To display this file a readable screen at a time, you enter

```
type setup.txt | more
```

You can also do this by entering

```
more < setup.txt
```

This time, DOS stops after displaying each screenful and waits before displaying the next screen until you press a key (any key).

MOVE

Moves one or more files to a new location on a disk. You can also use this DOS command to rename a directory on your disk.

Be careful! Moving a file to a location that contains a file with the same name will wipe out the existing file in that location.

DOSspeak

```
MOVE [drive:][path]filename
     [,[drive:][path]filename[...]] destination
     [/-y] [/y]
```

Variable or Option	Function
[drive:][path]filename	Specifies the drive, directory, and names of the file(s) to be moved or the name of the directory to be renamed. Instead of listing the files individually, separated with + signs, you can use wildcard characters in the filenames.
destination	Specifies the new location of the file(s) you're moving or the new name of the directory you're renaming. The *destination* parameter can consist of a drive letter and colon, directory name, or a combination of the two. If you want to rename a file or group of files, you can specify a *filename* parameter as well.
/-y	Forces the MOVE command to prompt you before overwriting an existing file.
/y	Allows the MOVE command to overwrite existing files without prompting.

Sample

Suppose that you want to move a file called BUNK.DOC that's currently in your C:\MYTURF directory to a new directory called C:\NEWSTUFF. To do so, enter

```
move c:\myturf\bunk.doc c:\newstuff
```

MSAV

Scans your computer for known viruses and then removes the viruses detected and/or reports back on them (available only in DOS 6 — not included in the Windows 98 version).

See also VSAFE, a DOS 6 command that continuously scans for viruses.

DOSspeak

```
MSAV [drive:] [/s] [/c] [/r] [/a] [/l] [/n] [/p]
     [/f] [/video]
```

Variable or Option	Function
drive:	Specifies the disk that you want MSAV to scan for viruses.
/s	Scans the disk specified by the *drive:* parameter but does not remove the viruses that it finds.
/c	Scans the disk specified by the *drive:* parameter and removes the viruses that it finds.
/r	Creates an MSAV.RPT file that lists the number of files MSAV checked, the number of viruses found, and the number of viruses removed. This report is placed in the root directory of the disk specified by the *drive:* parameter.
/a	Scans all drives except A or B.
/l	Scans all local drives except network drives.
/n	Displays the contents of the MSAV.TXT file, if this file is located in the same directory as the one that contains the MSAV.EXE file; then scans the disk specified by the *drive:* parameter. If MSAV finds a virus, it returns exit code 86 instead of displaying a message on your screen.
/p	Displays a command line instead of the normal GUI (graphical user interface) display.

Variable or Option	Function
/f	Turns off the display of names of the files that have been scanned. Use this switch only with the /n or /p switch.
/video	Sets the way the MSAV program is displayed on-screen.

You can specify any of the following as the /video parameter:

/video Parameter	Function
25	Sets the screen display to 25 lines (the default).
28	Sets the screen display to 28 lines (use with VGA graphics adapters).
43	Sets the screen display to 43 lines (use with EGA and VGA graphics adapters).
50	Sets the screen display to 50 lines (use with VGA graphics adapters only).
60	Sets the screen display to 60 lines (use with Video 7 graphics adapters only).
in	Runs MSAV in a color scheme even when a color display adapter is not detected.
bw	Runs MSAV in a black-and-white color scheme.
mono	Runs MSAV in a monochrome color scheme even when a color display adapter is detected.
lcd	Runs MSAV using shades of gray designed for a Liquid Crystal Display (LCD) screen.
ff	Specifies the fastest screen updating on computers using CGA (color/graphics) display adapters.
bf	Uses the computer's BIOS to display video.
nf	Disables the use of alternative fonts with the MSAV program.
bt	Enables the use of a mouse in Windows.
ngm	Runs MSAV displaying the mouse pointer (the arrow pointing left) instead of a graphics character (a rectangle).
le	Switches the left and right mouse buttons.
ps2	Resets the mouse if the mouse pointer disappears or locks up.

If you enter MSAV with no parameters, DOS loads MSAV and scans the current drive for known viruses.

Sample

To start MSAV in monochrome mode on your color monitor, scan drive C for any known viruses and remove them, and then list the files affected in a report, you enter

```
msav /c /r /mono
```

MSBACKUP

Runs the Microsoft Backup utility, a menu-driven program that enables you to back up your files without typing a single DOS command beyond MSBACKUP (sorry, only DOS 6 — and *not* the Windows 98 version — offers this utility!).

If you don't have Version 6, you can use the good old standby BACKUP command (yuk!) — *see* BACKUP. Note, however, that when you back up files with MSBACKUP, you must use the Microsoft Backup program to restore them.

DOSspeak

```
MSBACKUP [setup_file] [/bw | /lcd | /mda]
```

Variable or Option	Function
setup_file	Specifies the setup file that defines files to back up and the type of backup.
/bw	Starts the MS Backup program with a black-and-white screen.
/lcd	Starts the MS Backup program in shades of gray for a Liquid Crystal Display (LCD).
/mda	Starts MS Backup in a monochrome display.

Remember: The first time you use the MSBACKUP command, you must configure the program for your system. To do this configuration, you will need two or more floppy disks handy. Follow all the screen prompts closely, or better still, get someone who really understands DOS to do this part while you watch.

Sample

It's high time to do a full backup of your hard disk onto floppy disks. Now that you have DOS 6 on your system, you finally decide to bite the bullet. To back up your entire hard disk, you enter

```
msbackup
```

at the DOS prompt. Then follow these steps:

1. Press Alt+B at the first screen to select the Backup button.

2. At the main screen, press Alt+K and select [-C-] as the drive in the Backup From box.

3. Press Alt+Y and select Full as the Backup Type.

4. Press Alt+A and select the floppy drive letter and type of floppy disk to back up to.

5. Finally, put your first blank floppy disk in the backup drive and then press Alt+S to start the backup.

6. Follow the prompts and beeps as you feed disk after disk (you have a big hard drive).

7. After the backup is done, exit the Backup program by choosing the Quit button (press Alt+F, X if you're not at the first screen) to return to your old friend, the DOS prompt.

MSD (Diagnostics)

Starts the Microsoft Diagnostic utility that analyzes your system and tells you all sorts of neat stuff about it, such as how much memory your machine has, what version of DOS you're using, the type of video adapter you have, the number of disk drives you have, and the number of LPT (parallel) and COM (serial) ports you have (available in Versions 5+ only).

DOSspeak

MSD

Sample

You're using the 486 computer again (the Boss is in Outer Mongolia on business — what a job!), and you become curious about just how this PC is configured. To get the lowdown on the system, you enter

msd

NLSFUNC

(National Language Support Function) Gets DOS ready for code page switching (that is, using a foreign language character set).

You must use the NLSFUNC command before you use the CHCP (change code page) command to switch to a new code page. However, you only need to use it once per work session. If you have a Cousin Olaf (or some other reason to use code pages), you should put this command in your AUTOEXEC.BAT file.

DOSspeak

```
NLSFUNC [drive:][path][filename]
```

where [*drive:*][*path*][*filename*] specifies the drive, directory, and name of the file containing the country information (including such things as the time and date formats and currency symbol). If you omit the *drive:* and *path* parameters, DOS searches for this file in your DOS search path (**see** PATH). If you omit the *filename* parameter, DOS uses the COUNTRY.SYS file.

Sample

Cousin Olaf is in a funk because he can't get access to the Nordic code page with the CHCP 850 command. To remedy this situation, you remember that you first need to get DOS in the mood for code page switching by entering the command

```
nlsfunc
```

which promptly puts DOS in a National Language Support funk!

PATH

Specifies the search path where DOS is to look for all executable (command) files when you issue a DOS command or start an application program.

The PATH command that specifies all the directories and subdirectories you want in your search path is something you should put in your AUTOEXEC.BAT file; then DOS will establish this search path each time you power up your computer.

DOSspeak

```
PATH [drive:][path[;...]]
```

or

```
PATH [;]
```

Variable or Option	Function
drive:	Specifies the drive on which to set the search path. If you omit the *drive:* parameter, DOS assumes that you mean the current drive.
path	Specifies the directories and subdirectories to include in the search path.
;	Separates search paths. When used alone, it cancels the search path previously set with the PATH command.

If you enter PATH with no parameters, DOS displays the current search path.

Sample

You need to set the search path on your computer to include your \DOS and \123 directories so that the computer doesn't burp at you when you enter a particular DOS command or try to start 1-2-3 when you don't happen to be in the \DOS or \123 directory. To do so, you enter

```
path c:\dos;c:\123
```

POWER

Turns on and off the power management utility that sets the levels of power conservation and reports on its status. This command is useful when you're running a laptop computer on battery power (available only in DOS 6 — not included in the Windows 98 version).

You must use the DEVICE command in your CONFIG.SYS file to install the POWER.EXE device drive before you can use the POWER command (*see* DEVICE in Part V).

DOSspeak

```
POWER [adv[:max | reg | min]]
```

or

```
POWER std | off
```

Variable or Option	Function
adv[:max | reg | min]	Sets the power conservation setting when the computer's programs and hardware are idle. Specify max for maximum power conservation. Specify reg to balance power conservation with computer performance (the default). Specify min to maximize performance over power conservation.
std	Conserves power by using the power management features of your hardware if your computer supports the APM (Advanced Power Management) specification. If your computer doesn't support APM, this parameter turns off power management.
off	Turns off power management.

If you enter POWER without parameters, DOS displays the current power settings.

Sample

To turn on the power management on your laptop computer and maximize power conservation, you enter

```
power adv:max
```

PRINT

Prints a text file in the background so that you're free to use more DOS commands (what fun!). Not included in the Windows 98 version.

Don't use this command on a drive under the influence of the ASSIGN command. Also, don't issue it from a second copy of the DOS command interpreter (started with COMMAND) because it will probably cause your computer to crash and burn rather than your files to print.

DOSspeak

```
PRINT [/d:device] [/b:size] [/u:ticks] [/m:ticks2]
    [/s:ticks3] [/q:qsize] [/t][drive:][path]
    filename[...] [/c] [/p]
```

Variable or Option	Function
/d:device	Specifies the printer to use (default is PRN). The device parameter can be LPT1 through LPT3 or COM1 through COM4. If you omit the /d switch, DOS prompts you to enter the device name before printing.

Variable or Option	Function
/b:*size*	Specifies the size in bytes of the print buffer (default is 512K and the maximum size is 16,384K). The larger the buffer, the more files you can print and the less RAM you have free.
/u:*ticks*	Specifies the amount of time (the number of clock ticks) that the PRINT command waits for a busy printer before giving up its time slice (the default is 1, and the range is between 1 and 255).
/m:*ticks2*	Specifies the maximum amount of time (the number of clock ticks) that the PRINT command keeps control during its time slice (the default is 2, and the range is between 1 and 255).
/s:*ticks3*	Specifies the maximum number of time slices per second during which the PRINT command controls the operating system (the default is 8, and the range is between 1 and 255).
/q:*size*	Specifies the maximum number of files that the print queue can hold (the default is 10, and the range is between 1 and 32).
/t	Stops all printing and empties the print queue (if a file is printing when you give the PRINT command with this switch, DOS stops printing the page and advances the page to the next top of form).
[*drive:*][*path*]*filename*	Specifies the drive, directory, and name of the file(s) to print. To print multiple files, list the filenames separated by spaces or include wildcard characters in the *filename* parameter.
/c	Cancels the printing of the filename that precedes this /c switch, plus all subsequent filenames, until DOS encounters a filename followed by the /p switch.
/p	Adds the filename that precedes this /p switch, plus all subsequent filenames, until DOS encounters a filename followed by the /c switch.

If you enter PRINT with no other parameters, DOS displays a list of files in the print queue.

Sample

You have three files in your \MYTURF directory that you want to print from DOS: TWIDDLE.TXT, TWADDLE.TXT, and TATTLE.TXT. To print them in the background when \MYTURF is the current directory, you enter

```
print twiddle.txt twaddle.txt tattle.txt
```

After giving this command, you realize that you meant to print your TITTLE.TXT file instead of the TATTLE.TXT file. To remove TATTLE.TXT from the queue and print TITTLE.TXT instead, you then enter

```
print tattle.txt /c tittle.txt /p
```

PROMPT

Enables you to enhance the (fairly unhelpful) standard DOS prompt (you know, that bland A>, B>, C> thing) to something more exciting (or at least more informative).

If you come up with a favorite DOS prompt that you want to see day in and day out, put the PROMPT command in your AUTOEXEC.BAT file. Also, when creating a new prompt, add an extra space after the last character in the *text* parameter to separate it from the flashing underscore where you start entering your DOS command.

DOSspeak

```
PROMPT [text]
```

where *text* is composed of the following special $ characters or a combination of the text and these characters:

$ Character	What You Get for Your $
$t	The current time as returned by the TIME command.
$d	The current date as returned by the DATE command.
$p	The current drive and directory — for example, C:\MYTURF.
$v	The DOS version as returned by the VER command.
$n	The current drive letter, such as A or C (without the usual colon).
$g	The > character — for example, C> in the normal DOS prompt.
$l	The < character, which would change the normal DOS prompt to C< (ugh).
$b	The	(pipe) character, which would change the normal DOS prompt to C| (still not right . . .).
$q	The = (equal) sign, which would change the normal DOS prompt to C= (a little better).

$ Character	What You Get for Your $
$h	A backspace, which deletes whatever character precedes it in the *text* parameter.
$e	The Escape character (which appears on-screen as ¨).
$_ (underscore)	Places whatever follows in the *text* parameter on a new line; Use the $_ (make sure that you shift the hyphen) to create a prompt with two or more lines.
$$	Puts the dollar sign ($) in your DOS prompt.

If you enter the PROMPT command without a *text* parameter, DOS sets the prompt back to that bland old A>, B>, or C> thing.

Sample

You're tired of the cold and impersonal standard DOS prompt. You want to see something a little friendlier, such as

```
What's a gorgeous thing like you doing in a
      directory like C:\>?
```

To create this two-line DOS prompt on your computer, you enter

```
prompt What's a gorgeous thing like you doing!$_in
      a directory like $p$g?
```

Al in Finance doesn't feel that DOS shows him the proper respect, so he wants to change the DOS prompt to something a tad more courteous, such as

```
Master, what is thy bidding in directory C:\>?
```

To create this two-line prompt on his computer, he enters

```
prompt Master, what is thy bidding $_in directory
      $p$g?
```

QBASIC

Starts Microsoft QBasic, where you can code basic programs (you do want to be a programmer, don't you?). Not included in the Windows 98 version of DOS.

DOSspeak

```
QBASIC [/b] [/editor] [/g] [/h] [/mbf] [/nohi]
      [[/run] [drive:][path]filename]
```

Variable or Option	Function
/b	Forces QBasic to be displayed in monochrome on a color monitor (helpful if you're coding on a laptop with an LCD screen).
/editor	Starts the DOS Editor — *see* EDIT.
/g	Provides fastest-possible screen response when running QBasic with a CGA (color/graphics) adapter.
/h	Displays the maximum number of lines possible on your monitor.
/mbf	Causes numbers to be read and stored in Microsoft binary format.
/nohi	Suppresses the display of high-intensity video while using QBasic (don't use this one on laptops because it routinely causes them to have seizures and crash).
/run	Causes QBasic to run the QBasic file specified by the *filename* parameter before loading it into the Editor.
[*drive:*][*path*]*filename*	Specifies the drive, directory, and the name of an existing QBasic file that you either want to run (with the /run switch) or edit, or the new QBasic file that you want to code.

If you enter QBASIC with no parameters, DOS starts the QBasic editing screen, where you can press Enter to see the Survival Guide (sounds like fun, huh?) or press Esc to start coding a new QBasic program.

Sample

Like it or not, you have this bizarre urge to *program in Basic* that you just can't control! Finally, you give in to this perverse craving and start work on a new program file called MYPROG.BAS. To create this file when you start the QBasic program, you enter the command

```
qbasic myprog
```

This command starts the QBasic program and puts you in a new file called MYPROG.BAS (the program automatically appends the BAS extension to the filename), where you can now indulge yourself in this sordid "coding" thing till the cows come home.

RD or RMDIR

Deletes an empty directory from a disk. DOS will accept RMDIR instead of RD, if you're really into typing.

No matter how you enter this command, be very careful with it because there is no way to undelete a deleted directory. If you do take out a directory in error, you have to restore it from backup disks (*see* BACKUP and RESTORE) or re-create it (*see* MD or MKDIR).

DOSspeak

RD [*drive:*]*path*

Variable or Option	Function
drive:	Specifies the drive that contains the disk with the directory you want to get rid of. If you omit this parameter, DOS assumes that you mean the current drive.
path	Specifies the name of the directory that you want to get rid of. You must specify this parameter, and the directory you specify must be empty of all files and subdirectories before RD can do its stuff.

Sample

You finally decide that it's time to get rid of your NONSENSE directory (as you long ago got rid of the nonsense that was in it). To delete this now empty, unused, and unloved subdirectory of the \MYTURF directory on your hard disk, you enter

    rd nonsense

Unfortunately, when you press Enter, you get this really ambiguous error message Invalid path, not directory, or directory not empty (talk about hedging your bets). You look at the DOS prompt and realize the error of your ways: The NONSENSE directory is the current directory. Because DOS can't remove a directory while you're in it, you type cd . . to go up a level to the \MYTURF directory. Now when you repeat your RD command, it works like a charm.

RECOVER

Recovers files that have bad sectors or reconstructs files from a disk that has a damaged directory structure (versions prior to Version 6 only).

Don't be misled — although RECOVER sounds innocuous enough, it can wreak havoc on your disk if applied to files that aren't already trashed. Therefore, don't play around with the RECOVER command and don't confuse it with the RESTORE command that you use when you need to copy files onto the disk from which they were backed up. Also, don't use RECOVER on a disk under the influence of the JOIN or SUBST command and don't try to use it on a network drive.

DOSspeak

RECOVER [*drive:*][*path*]*filename*

or

RECOVER *drive:*

Variable or Option	Function
[*drive:*][*path*]*filename*	Specifies the drive, directory, and name of the file to recover.
drive:	Specifies the disk that you want reconstructed.

Beware! In the earliest versions of DOS, if you enter RECOVER with no parameters, DOS assumes that you want to recover all the files on the current drive (which often is your hard disk, drive C, and could result in a really big, bad mess).

REN or RENAME

Renames a file or group of files.

DOS will accept RENAME as the command name if you prefer it over the REN abbreviation.

Windows 98 allows you to use the RENAME command to rename directories, too!

DOSspeak

REN [*drive:*][*path*]*filename1 filename2*

Variable or Option	Function
[*drive:*][*path*]*filename1*	Specifies the drive, directory, and name of the file that you want to rename. If you omit the *drive:* and *path* parameters, DOS assumes that the file is in the current drive. To rename multiple files, use wildcard characters in the *filename1* parameter.

Variable or Option	Function
filename2	Specifies the new name for the file. When renaming multiple files, use wildcard characters in the *filename2* parameter. You cannot, however, include a *drive:* and a *path* parameter with *filename2* — the renamed file must remain in the same location. (Use COPY when you want to both rename and relocate a file.)

Sample

You have a file named HILUCRE.WK1 in your \123STUFF directory that you want to rename BIGBUCKS.WK1. To rename it while you're in your \MYTURF directory, you enter

```
ren c:\123stuff\hilucre.wk1 bigbucks.wk1
```

REPLACE

Selectively adds or replaces files from one disk or directory to another. Not included in the Windows 98 version of DOS.

Before using this command, make sure that the file you're about to overwrite is one that you're comfortable deleting.

DOSspeak

```
REPLACE [drive1:][path1]filename [drive2:][path2]
        [/a] [/p] [/r] [/s] [/w] [/u]
```

Variable or Option	Function
[*drive1:*][*path1*]*filename*	Specifies the drive, path, and name of the source files (that is, the files that you want to replace or add to those in the destination directory). To specify multiple files, use wildcard characters in the *filename* parameter.
[*drive2:*]*path2*	Specifies the destination drive and directory where the source files should overwrite or be added to those already there.
/a	Adds new source files that do not already exist in the destination directory. You can't use this switch with the /s or /u switch.
/p	Tells DOS to prompt you for confirmation before replacing a file in the destination directory with a source file.

(continued)

Variable or Option	Function
/r	Specifies that read-only files in the destination directory can be replaced.
/s	Specifies that files in all subdirectories of the destination directory be replaced.
/w	Pauses the REPLACE command until you press any key, giving you the opportunity to switch disks or insert a disk in the drive specified by the *drive1:* parameter.
/u	(Versions 4+) Specifies that DOS replace only those files in the destination directory that are older than their counterparts in the source drive. (In versions prior to 4, you use /d instead of /u.) You can't use this switch with the /a switch.

Sample

Al in Finance has given you a floppy disk with all sorts of worksheet files on it. You want to copy only those files that are not already in your \123STUFF directory or that have a more recent revision date. To do this task, you first enter

```
replace a:\*.wk1 c:\123stuff /a
```

to have DOS copy only those files on Al's floppy disk that don't already exist in your \123STUFF directory. Next, you enter

```
replace a:\*.wk1 c:\123stuff /u /p
```

to have DOS replace your files only when the files on Al's floppy disk are more recent, as well as to prompt you before replacing each one.

RESTORE

Restores files backed up with the BACKUP command (versions prior to Version 6).

If you used the MSBACKUP command in DOS 6, you can't use the RESTORE command to restore your backup files. Instead, you must use the Microsoft Backup program.

Before using this command, make sure that the files to be replaced are ones that you're comfortable deleting.

DOSspeak

```
RESTORE drive1: drive2:[path[filename]] [/s] [/p]
    [/b:date] [/a:date] [/e:time] [/l:time] [/m]
    [/n] [d]
```

Variable or Option	Function
drive1:	Specifies the drive containing the floppy disk with the backup files.
drive2:[*path*[*filename*]]	Specifies the drive, directory, and name of the file(s) that will be restored. If you omit the *drive2:* parameter, DOS assumes that you mean the current drive. If you include a *path* parameter, you must also include a *filename* parameter (which can include wildcard characters when you're specifying multiple files to be restored). The *path* parameter must match the directory from which the files were originally backed up.
/s	Specifies that files in all subdirectories of the destination directory be replaced.
/p	Tells DOS to prompt you for confirmation before restoring read-only files or files that have been revised since they were last backed up.
/b:*date*	Specifies that DOS restore only files modified on or before the *date* parameter (*mm-dd-yy* is the default format).
/a:*date*	Specifies that DOS restore only files modified on or after the *date* parameter (*mm-dd-yy* is the default format).
/e:*time*	Specifies that DOS restore only files modified at or before the *time* parameter (*hh:mm:ss* is the default format).
/l:*time*	Specifies that DOS restore only files modified at or later than the *time* parameter (*hh:mm:ss* is the default format).
/m	Specifies that DOS restore only those files that have been modified since they were backed up.
/n	Specifies that DOS restore only those files that have been deleted since they were backed up.
/d	(Versions 5+) Specifies that DOS display the names of all the files on the backup disk that match the *filename* parameter, without actually restoring them.

Sample

You've backed up the files in your \123STUFF directory on a floppy disk, and now, due to an unfortunate encounter with the DEL command, you need to restore all the files on the backup disk that are no longer in your \123STUFF directory. To do so, you put the backup disk in drive A and then enter

```
restore a:\*.* c:\123stuff /n
```

SCANDISK

Checks a disk for boo-boos and, if possible, fixes them. This nifty command can fix problems with the file allocation table (your so-called FAT table), file system structure (lost clusters and cross-linked files), directory tree, DoubleSpace compression (*see* DBLSPACE), and the MS-DOS boot sector.

In DOS 6.2, SCANDISK replaces the venerable CHKDSK command (you guys using earlier versions of DOS still need to rely on good old CHKDSK).

You can't use the SCANDISK command to check a CD-ROM or network drive, nor to check a drive under the influence of the ASSIGN, JOIN, or SUBST command or one created with the INTERLNK command. Also, don't try to use SCANDISK to check and repair a disk when other programs are running.

DOSspeak

To check and repair the current drive:

```
SCANDISK
```

To check a noncurrent drive or all drives:

```
SCANDISK [drive:[drive:...] | /ALL] [/CHECKONLY |
    AUTOFIX [/NOSAVE] | /CUSTOM] [/SURFACE] [/MONO]
    [/NOSUMMARY]
```

To check an unmounted DriveSpace compressed drive:

```
SCANDISK volume-name [/CHECKONLY | AUTOFIX
    [/NOSAVE] | /CUSTOM] [/MONO] [/NOSUMMARY]
```

To check files for fragmentation:

```
SCANDISK /FRAGMENT [drive:][path]filename
```

To undo repairs made previously with SCANDISK:

```
SCANDISK /UNDO [undo-drive:] [/MONO]
```

Variable or Option	Function
[drive:][drive:]	Specifies the drive and directory to check and repair.
[drive:][path]filename	Specifies the drive, directory path, and file(s) to check for fragmentation. You can include the * and ? wildcard characters in the *filename* parameter to check all files whose names fit the general pattern.

Variable or Option	Function
volume-name	Specifies the name of the unmounted DriveSpace volume that you want to check and repair.
undo-drive:	Specifies the drive containing the Undo disk so you can undo repairs that you just made with ScanDisk.
/ALL	Checks and repairs all local (actually attached) drives on your computer.
/CHECKONLY	Checks for errors on the specified drive(s) but does not attempt to repair any errors.
/AUTOFIX	Fixes errors that are located during checking without asking your permission (this is the default way of doing business for ScanDisk).
/NOSAVE	Deletes lost clusters located during the scan instead of saving them as files. This switch can only be used together with the /AUTOFIX switch. If you run ScanDisk with the /AUTOFIX switch but without the /NOSAVE switch, DOS saves the lost clusters as files in the root directory.
/CUSTOM	Runs ScanDisk using the configuration settings that are found in the CUSTOM section of your SCANDISK.INI file (and you didn't even know you had one!).
/SURFACE	Performs a surface scan of the specified drive(s). In scanning an uncompressed drive, ScanDisk lets you know that data can be reliably written and read from the disk. In scanning a compressed drive, ScanDisk lets you know that its data can be successfully uncompressed.
/MONO	Tells ScanDisk to display the checking information for a monochrome monitor. Instead of wasting time setting this switch each time you use the SCANDISK command, you accomplish the same thing by putting the line DISPLAY=MONO in your SCANDISK.INI file (now that you know you have one).
/NOSUMMARY	Stops ScanDisk from displaying a summary after checking each drive and stops Scan Disk from prompting you to supply an Undo disk when it finds errors.

Sample

Suppose that Al in Finance gives you a really lame-looking diskette and you want to know whether any of its data is still intact. To check this disk and fix any problems, put the disk in drive A and enter

```
SCANDISK A:
```

Suppose that you want to check your hard drive with ScanDisk without having any of the problems fixed. To do so when C is the default directory, enter

```
SCANDISK /CHECKONLY
```

SET

Creates, deletes, or modifies the value assigned to a DOS environment variable.

 This command is safe only in the hands of a programmer or some other totally DOSsed person. Stay clear unless they give you hazard pay.

DOSspeak

```
SET [variable=[string]]
```

Variable or Option	Function
variable	Specifies the name of the variable to create, edit, or delete.
string	Specifies the value to be assigned to your variable. To delete a variable, you omit the *string* parameter.

If you enter SET with no parameters, DOS lists the current values assigned to your environment variables.

Sample

Today, you need your directory listings to be sorted in descending date order (from the most recent to the least recent), with subdirectories preceding files. Rather than type `dir /o:g-d` each time, you assign the sorting switch that gives you the preferred order to the variable DIRCMD used by the DIR command (in Versions 5+). To do so, you enter

```
set dircmd=/o:g-d
```

Now DOS automatically sorts the directory listings in your preferred order any time you use the DIR command during the current work session. If later you decide to return to the standard directory listing, you delete the DIRCMD variable by entering

```
set dircmd=
```

SETVER

Sets the version number that DOS reports to a particular program (available in Versions 5+).

Note: Assigning a new DOS version number to a program has no effect on the program's system requirements. If a particular program requires DOS 5 to run, using SETVER to set the DOS version number to 4.0 doesn't make the program run under this earlier version of DOS.

This command is safe only in the hands of a programmer or some other totally DOSsed person. Stay clear unless they give you hazard pay.

DOSspeak

SETVER [*drive:path*]*filename n.nn*

or

SETVER [*drive:path*]*filename* [/delete [/quiet]]

Variable or Option	Function
[*drive:path*]	Specifies the drive and directory that contains the SETVER.EXE file that updates the table of applications. If you omit this parameter, DOS assumes the current drive and directory.
filename	Specifies the name of the executable file that you want to add to the table of applications.
n.nn	Specifies the DOS version number that you want assigned to the file specified by the *filename* parameter in the table of applications.
/delete	Removes the file specified by the *filename* parameter from the table of applications. You can abbreviate this switch to /d.
/quiet	Suppresses the display of all messages when deleting a file (must be used with the /delete or /d switch).

If you enter SETVER with no parameters, DOS displays the contents of the table of applications.

SHARE

Enables file-sharing and locking capabilities on a hard disk.

This command is used in some network environments and with Windows. It is not included in the Windows 98 version of DOS, however.

This command is safe only in the hands of a programmer or some other totally DOSsed person. Stay clear unless they give you hazard pay.

DOSspeak

SHARE [/f:*space*] [/l:*locks*]

Variable or Option	Function
/f:*space*	Specifies how much memory (in bytes) to allocate for file-sharing information (the default is 2048).
/l:*locks*	Specifies how many files can be locked at one time (the default is 20).

If you enter SHARE with no parameters, DOS loads the Share program into memory by using the default values.

SMARTDRV

Starts or configures the SMARTDrive program, which sets up a disk cache in extended memory for speeding up various disk operations (Versions 6+).

Don't use the SMARTDRV command after you've started Windows.

For SMARTDrive to use extended memory, your CONFIG.SYS file must contain a DEVICE command that loads the HIMEM.SYS driver or another driver that manages extended memory. Also, to do double buffering that provides compatibility for hard-disk control-lers that can't work with the memory provided by EMM386 device driver or Windows running in 386-enhanced mode, you need to add a DEVICE command to your CONFIG.SYS file that loads SMARTDRV.EXE. *See* DEVICE in Part V for details.

DOSspeak

To start SMARTDrive and configure a disk cache from either your AUTOEXEC.BAT file or the DOS prompt:

```
[drive:] [path] SMARTDRV [/x] [[drive[+|-]]...]
    [/u] [/c | /r] [/f | /n] [/l] [/v | /q | /s]
    [initcachesize[wincachesize]] [/e:elementsize]
    [/b:buffersize]
```

After SMARTDrive is running, to have the program write all cached information to a cached disk or to clear the contents of the existing cache and restart the program:

```
SMARTDRV [[drive[+ | -]]... [/c] [/r]
```

Variable or Option	Function
[drive:]path	Specifies the location of the SMARTDRV.EXE file. If you omit these parameters, DOS assumes that this file is in the search path (*see* PATH).
drive[+ | -]	Specifies the letter of the disk(s) that you want to cache. If you specify a drive without a plus or minus sign, DOS enables read-caching while disabling write-caching. If you add a plus sign, DOS enables both read- and write-caching for the specified drive. If you add a minus sign, DOS disables both read- and write-caching for the specified drive. If you omit the drive parameter, floppy disks created with Interlnk (*see* INTERLNK) are read-cached but not write-cached, while hard disk drives on your system are both read- and write-cached. To specify multiple drives, separate drive letters with a space.
/e:elementsize	Specifies the amount of cache (in bytes) that SMARTDrive moves at a time. The *elementsize* parameter can be any of the following values: 1024, 2048, 4096, or 8192 (the default).
initcachesize	Specifies the size of the cache (in kilobytes) when SMARTDrive starts and Windows isn't running. If you omit this parameter, SMARTDrive sets the value according to how much memory your computer has (see the following table).
wincachesize	Specifies how much SMARTDrive reduces the cache size (in kilobytes) to recover memory necessary for running Windows. If you omit this parameter, SMARTDrive sets the value according to how much memory your computer has (see the following table). If you specify an *initcachesize* parameter that is smaller than the *wincachesize* parameter, DOS sets the *initcachesize* to the *wincachesize*.
/b:buffersize	Specifies the size of the read-ahead buffer. The *buffersize* parameter can be set to any multiple of the elementsize parameter.

(continued)

Variable or Option	Function
/c	Writes all cached information to the appropriate cached disk. Use this option prior to turning off your computer to ensure that all cached information is saved on disk (you need not use this switch before rebooting with Ctrl+Alt+Delete, only prior to manually shutting down or pressing the Reset button).
/r	Clears the contents of the existing cache and restarts SMARTDrive.
/l	Prevents SMARTDrive from automatically loading into the upper memory blocks (UMBs) even when these blocks are available.
/q	Instructs SMARTDrive not to display status messages when the program starts (only if the program encounters an error when starting). You can't use this switch with the /v switch.
/v	Instructs SMARTDrive to display status messages along with error messages when it starts. You can't use this switch with the /q switch.
/s	Displays additional information about the status of SMARTDrive.
/x	Disables the write-behind caching on all new drives.
/u	Instructs SMARTDRV not to load the CD-ROM caching module, even if you have a CD-ROM drive.
/f	Causes SMARTDrive to write the cached data after each command completes (the default mode).
/n	Instructs SMARTDrive to write the cached data when the system is idle.

The following table shows the default values for the *initcachesize* and *wincachesize* parameters, depending on the amount of extended memory.

Extended Memory	Default initcachesize	Default wincachesize
Up to 1MB	All extended memory	Zero (no caching)
Up to 2MB	1MB	256K
Up to 4MB	1MB	512K
Up to 6MB	2MB	1MB
Over 6MB	2MB	2MB

If you enter SMARTDRV with no parameters, DOS sets up a disk cache using the default values.

Sample

To set up a disk cache with the default size of 1MB on a computer that has 2MB of extended memory total each time you start your computer, you add the following command to your AUTOEXEC.BAT file:

```
c:\dos\smartdrv
```

To ensure that cached information is saved to disk before you shut down your computer, enter at the DOS prompt

```
smartdrv /c
```

SORT

Sorts lines of text and writes the results to the screen, a file, or another device.

DOSspeak

```
SORT [/r] [/+n] < [drive1:][path1]filename1
    [> [drive2:][path2]filename2]
```

or

```
[command |] SORT [/r] [/+n]
    [drive2:][path2]filename2]
```

Variable or Option	Function
/r	Reverses the normal sort order (A to Z and then 0 to 9 — called *ascending order*) to Z to A and then 9 to 0 (called *descending order*).
/+n	Sorts the lines by the characters in the number of the column specified by the *n* parameter. If you omit this switch, DOS sorts the text according to the characters in the first column.
[drive1:][path1]filename1	Specifies the drive, directory, and name of the file to be sorted.
[drive2:][path2]filename2	Specifies the drive, directory, and name of the file where the sorted output is to be saved.
command	Specifies the DOS command whose output is to be sorted.

If you enter the SORT command with no parameters, DOS sorts the lines of text that you type at the keyboard (each line separated by a carriage return) according to the character in the first column, as soon as you press Ctrl+Z or F6 and press Enter.

Sample

To sort a list of CEOs for client companies saved in a file called
CEOS.TXT in your \MYTURF directory by the first character of
their names and store the sorted names in a file called
CEOSORT.TXT on a disk in drive A, you enter

```
sort \myturf\ceos.txt a:\ceosort.txt
```

To sort the output of a directory listing in descending order by
filename, you enter

```
dir | sort /r
```

SUBST

Associates a drive letter with a directory, making the directory
into what's known as a *virtual drive* (as opposed to a real, physical
drive on your computer, such as A or C).

You can't use the SUBST command on a drive under the influence
of any of the following DOS commands: ASSIGN, BACKUP,
CHKDISK, DISKCOMP, DISKCOPY, FASTOPEN, FDISK, FORMAT,
LABEL, RECOVER, RESTORE, or SYS.

This command is safe only in the hands of a programmer or some
other totally DOSsed person. Stay clear unless they give you
hazard pay.

DOSspeak

SUBST [*drive1:* [*drive2:*]*path*]

or

SUBST *drive1:* /d

Variable or Option	Function
drive1:	Specifies the letter of the virtual drive that you want to assign to the specified directory.
[*drive2:*]*path*	Specifies the physical drive and directory that is to be assigned to the virtual drive.
/d	Deletes the virtual drive specified by the *drive1:* parameter.

If you enter SUBST with no other parameters, DOS displays a list of
all virtual drives currently assigned.

Sample

To be able to refer to your \MYTURF directory on drive C as drive D, you enter

```
subst d: c:\myturf
```

Then to check the status of your new virtual drive D, you enter

```
subst
```

and DOS displays the current substitution status as

```
D: => C:\MYTURF
```

When you're ready to delete this virtual drive, you enter

```
subst d: /d
```

SYS

Transfers the DOS system files to a specified disk so that you can boot your computer with that disk.

DOSspeak

```
SYS [drive1:][path] drive2:
```

Variable or Option	Function
drive1:[path]	Specifies the drive and directory containing the DOS system files. In Versions 4+, if you omit these parameters, DOS assumes that you mean the current directory.
drive2:	Specifies the drive containing the disk onto which you want to copy the system files. This disk must be formatted but have no files on it.

Sample

You just formatted a floppy disk in drive A but forgot to use the /s switch to copy the system files onto it so that in an emergency (that is, when DOS can't find your hard disk), you could use it to boot the computer. To copy the system files, you enter

```
sys c: a:
```

After copying these files, you use the COPY command to copy the COMMAND.COM file to the floppy disk in drive A (this step is unnecessary in DOS 5 and later versions).

TIME

Displays and changes the current time used by DOS and application programs to add the time stamp to files.

DOSspeak

`TIME [hh:mm[:ss[.xx]]] [a | p]`

Variable or Option	Function
hh	Specifies the hours based on a 24-hour clock (0 to 23, where 0 represents 12 midnight).
:mm	Specifies the minutes (between 0 and 59). If you omit the *:mm* parameter, DOS uses 0 minutes.
:ss	Specifies the number of seconds (between 0 and 59). If you omit the *:ss* parameter, DOS uses 0 seconds.
.xx	Specifies the hundredths of seconds (between 0 and 99). If you omit the *.xx* parameter, DOS uses 0 hundredths.
a | p	(Versions 5+) Specifies a.m. or p.m. when using a COUNTRY code whose date format supports a 12-hour clock (as does the U.S. default).

Enter TIME with no parameters to display the current time setting.

Sample

It's the Monday morning right after you've changed all the clocks at home to Daylight Saving Time. To see what time your computer thinks it is, you enter

`time`

and press Enter. According to your watch, it's now 10:30 a.m., but your computer still thinks it's 9:30 a.m. To get your computer's clock up to date, you enter

`time 10:30`

TREE

Displays a diagram showing the directory structure of the specified disk or path. Not included in the Windows 98 version of DOS.

DOSspeak

`TREE [drive:][path] [/f] [/a]`

Variable or Option	Function
drive:	Specifies the drive whose directory structure is to be displayed. If you omit the *drive:* parameter, DOS assumes the current drive.
path	Specifies the topmost directory to be included in the diagram. If you omit the *path* parameter, DOS displays the entire directory structure of the disk specified by the *drive:* parameter.
/f	Displays the name of each file in the directory included in the diagram.
/a	Displays the diagram with text (ASCII) characters rather than with graphics characters (which your printer may not be able to reproduce).

If you enter TREE with no parameters, DOS displays the directory structure of the current drive, starting with the current directory.

Sample

You need to figure out in which directory Sue keeps her 1-2-3 worksheet files because she's home sick and you're stuck doing her spreadsheets today. To display the directory structure of her hard disk one screenful at a time, you enter

```
tree c: | more
```

After examining the structure (and locating the whereabouts of her worksheet files C:\123\SUESHEET), you decide it would be good to have a printout of this diagram for later reference. Because Sue's old printer doesn't support graphics characters, you need to turn off the graphics when you print this diagram by entering

```
tree c: /a > prn
```

TYPE

Displays the contents of a text file on-screen.

If you use the TYPE command in attempting to display a nontext file (such as a 1-2-3 worksheet or something like that) instead of numbers and stuff that you can read, strange hieroglyphics appear, accompanied by spasmodic beeps. If these events happen, don't worry — you haven't screwed up the file or anything like that. The signals just mean that the file's information is stored in some sort of binary format that invariably gives the TYPE command indigestion.

DOSspeak

TYPE [*drive:*][*path*]*filename*

Variable or Option	Function
[*drive:*]*path*	Specifies the drive and directory containing the file whose contents you want displayed. If you omit the drive and path, DOS assumes that the file is in the current drive and directory.
filename	Specifies the name of the text file whose contents you want displayed.

Sample

You've just gotten a new program that contains a READ.ME text file on the first disk. To see whether it contains anything that you should pay any attention to, you display its text on-screen by entering

```
type a:read.me
```

Unfortunately, a whole bunch of warnings and stuff like that fly by in a blur that you can't possibly read. So this time, you display the file a screenful at a time by entering

```
type a:read.me | more
```

UNDELETE

Restores files deleted by mistake with the DEL or ERASE command (available in Versions 5 through 6.22 only).

Remember: Be sure to use the UNDELETE command as soon as you discover that you blew off a file by mistake. If you continue to work (especially when moving and copying other files around), DOS may use the deleted file's space for other files, making it impossible for this command to work its magic.

DOSspeak

UNDELETE [*drive:*][*path*][*filename*] [/dt | /ds |dos]

or

UNDELETE [/list | /all | /purge[*drive*] | /status |
    /load | /unload | /s[*drive*] | /t[*drive*]
    [*-entries*]]

Variable or Option	Function
[*drive:*][*path*]*filename*	Specifies the disk, directory, and name of the file(s) that you want to undelete. To undelete multiple files, use wildcard characters in the *filename* parameter.
/list	Lists all the files that you can undelete without prompting you to undelete them.
/all	Undeletes all specified files without prompting you.
/dt	Undeletes only files included in the deletion-tracking file produced by the MIRROR command (the default when a deletion-tracking file exists).
/dos	Undeletes only files listed as deleted by DOS (the default when a deletion-tracking file doesn't exist).
/ds	(Version 6) Recovers files protected by Delete Sentry.
/purge[*drive*]	(Version 6) Purges all files in the Delete Sentry directory.
/status	(Version 6) Displays the protection method in effect for each drive.
/load	(Version 6) Loads the Undelete memory-resident program.
/unload	(Version 6) Unloads the Undelete memory-resident program.
/s[*drive*]	(Version 6) Enables the Delete Sentry method of protection and loads the memory-resident portion of the Undelete program. The *drive* parameter specifies the drive where DOS records the recovery information. If you omit the *drive* parameter, DOS assumes that you mean the current drive.
/t*drive*	(Version 6) Loads the deletion-tracking program for the *drive* specified after the /t switch. This program saves information each time you delete a file in the specified *drive* in a special file called PCTRACKR.DEL, which is located in the root directory of the *drive*.
-*entries*	(Version 6) Specifies the number of entries that the deletion-tracking program will save. Default values for the -*entries* parameter vary according to the size of the disk specified by the *drive* parameter (*see* the table in the MIRROR entry).

If you enter UNDELETE with no parameters, DOS lists those files in the current drive and directory that can be undeleted and prompts you to undelete each one.

Sample

The moment you press Enter, it hits you that instead of deleting the obsolete version of a file, you just eighty-sixed the version you spent the last two hours editing (you should have typed the filename BIGDOC1.TXT but entered BIGDOC2.TXT instead). To get this deleted file back and avoid having to redo all the work, you enter

```
undelete bigdoc1.txt
```

DOS then displays the name of the file as

```
?IGDOC2 TXT
```

and prompts you to undelete it. When you press Y, DOS next prompts you to type the first character of the filename. After pressing B and then Enter, you see that wonderfully reassuring message `File successfully undeleted` right above the now-beautiful DOS prompt.

UNFORMAT

Rebuilds the directory structure and restores the files on a disk that was erased with the FORMAT command (available in Versions 5 through 6.22 only).

Note: UNFORMAT can't restore a disk that has been formatted with the FORMAT command's /u (unconditional) switch, nor can it restore a network drive. Keep in mind that you need to use UNFORMAT to restore the data on a disk before you put any files on the newly (and mistakenly) formatted disk. Also be aware that UNFORMAT is best at rebuilding subdirectories and restoring their files (files in the root directory of the disk are often irretrievable) and that this command is much more successful with a disk containing file and directory information recorded with the MIRROR command.

DOSspeak

UNFORMAT *drive:* [/u] [/l] [/test] [/p]

or

UNFORMAT *drive:* [/j]

or

UNFORMAT /partn [/l]

Variable or Option	Function
drive:	Specifies the disk whose contents you want to rebuild.
/j	(Version 5 only) Compares the contents of files created by the MIRROR command with the system information without rebuilding the structure or restoring the files.
/u	(Version 5 only) Rebuilds the directory structure and restores the files on the specified disk without using the file information recorded with the MIRROR command.
/l	Lists all the file and directory names on the specified disk and then prompts you to use this information to rebuild the disk. When used with the /partn switch, DOS displays the partition table of a hard disk but does not rebuild the disk.
/test	Lists all the file and directory names on the specified disk but does not rebuild the disk.
/p	Sends the UNFORMAT messages to the printer connected to LPT1.
/partn	(Version 5 only) Restores the partition tables of a hard disk, provided that you don't use this switch with /l and that DOS finds the PARTNSAV.FIL created with the MIRROR command's /partn switch.

Sample

Your very agitated Boss comes to you looking for an unlabeled high-density disk that was "right there on the desk" earlier this morning. According to the Boss, this disk contains the only copies of the budget worksheet files that the president of the company wants right after lunch today. Suddenly, you realize that the unmarked high-density disk that you "borrowed" from the Boss's office earlier and just finished FORMATting is the one that's "lost"! In an attempt to resuscitate the Boss's trashed budget files and save your job, you put the newly formatted (but still empty) disk in drive A and enter

```
unformat a:
```

Fortunately for all (especially *you* because you really need this job), your Boss wisely saved the budget worksheets in a subdirectory called \WHATIF, and the UNFORMAT command is able to completely rebuild this directory and everything in it.

VER

Displays the version of DOS that you're running on your computer.

DOSspeak

ver

Sample

Today, you're using Cindy's computer. However, you don't remember what version of DOS she has on her machine (and you want to make sure that she has at least Version 5, with the UNDELETE and UNFORMAT commands, before you mess with any of her files). To find out what the DOS version is, you enter

ver

VERIFY

Turns on or off the switch that controls disk-write verification used with commands such as COPY and DISKCOPY to check whether data was written correctly to a disk.

You can also turn on disk-write verification by adding the /v switch when you are using the COPY or DISKCOPY command.

DOSspeak

VERIFY [on | off]

where the on parameter turns on disk-write verification and the off parameter turns off disk-write verification. If you enter VERIFY without one of these parameters, DOS displays the current disk-write verification (the default is off).

Sample

To turn on disk-write verification before you begin copying a bunch of files, you enter

verify on

Then, later in the day, to verify that disk-write verification is still on before you do more copying, you enter

verify

VOL

Displays the current volume label and serial number assigned to a specified disk.

For information on how to add, change, or delete a volume label, *see* LABEL.

DOSspeak

VOL [*drive:*]

where *drive:* specifies the disk for which you want the volume label. If you omit the *drive:* parameter, DOS displays the volume label of the current drive.

Sample

You're looking for a high-density floppy disk with the volume label VITAL STUFF. To see whether the unlabeled disk you just picked out of a heap on your desk is the one you want, you put the disk in drive A and enter

vol a:

Unfortunately, this disk proves not to be the one you're looking for; its volume label is PETTY STUFF. Better luck next disk!

VSAFE

Continuously monitors your computer for any nasty computer viruses and displays a warning should one be detected (available in DOS 6 only — not in the Windows 98 version).

VSAFE is a terminate-and-stay-resident (TSR) program that uses about 22K of memory.

Don't use the VSAFE command when you are running Microsoft Windows on your computer.

DOSspeak

VSAFE [/*option*[+ | -]...] [/ne] [/nx] [/A*x* | /C*x*]
    [/n] [/d] [/u]

Variable or Option	Function
/option[+ | -]	Specifies how DOS monitors for viruses (see the following table for possible values). To turn on an option, follow the option value with a + (plus). To turn off an option, follow the option value with a - (minus or hyphen). To specify multiple /option parameters, separate them with a space.
/ne	Prevents DOS from loading VSAFE into expanded RAM memory.
/nx	Prevents DOS from loading VSAFE into extended RAM memory.
/Ax	Sets Alt plus the letter you specify for the x parameter as the hot keys that display the VSAFE screen.
/Cx	Sets Ctrl plus the letter you specify for the x parameter as the hot keys that display the VSAFE screen.
/n	Enables VSAFE to check for viruses on network drives.
/d	Turns off checksumming.
/u	Removes VSAFE from memory.

The VSAFE /option parameters can include any of the following:

VSAFE Option	Function
1	Warns of formatting that could completely erase the hard disk (the default is on).
2	Warns of an attempt by the program to remain in memory (the default is off).
3	Prevents programs from writing to disk (the default is off).
4	Checks the executable files that DOS opens (the default is on).
5	Checks all disks for boot sector viruses (the default is on).
6	Warns of attempts to write to the boot sector or partition of a hard disk (the default is on).
7	Warns of attempts to write to the boot sector of a floppy disk (the default is off).
8	Warns of attempts to modify executable files (the default is off).

If you enter VSAFE with no parameters, DOS loads the VSAFE program using the default values.

Sample

Al in Finance just called — Sue's computer picked up such a bad virus that they couldn't save any of the data on her hard disk. Now that you've got DOS 6 on your system, you decide it's time to monitor your computer for viruses. To turn on virus monitoring and make Alt+V the VSAFE hot keys, you enter

```
vsafe /Av
```

XCOPY

Selectively copies files, including the files in subdirectories, if you want to include them.

DOSspeak

```
XCOPY source [destination] [/a | /m] [/d:date] [/p]
      [/s [/e]] [/v] [/w] [/-y] [/y]
```

Variable or Option	Function
source	Specifies the drive, directory, and name of the source files (that is, the ones to copy). If you specify only a drive, DOS copies all the files in the specified drive. If you specify a path without a filename, DOS copies all the files in the specified directory of the current drive. To copy multiple files, use wildcard characters when specifying the filename.
destination	Specifies the drive, directory, and/or new names of the destination files. If you omit the *destination* parameter, DOS assumes that you mean the current drive and directory and does not rename the copied files.
/a	Copies source files that have their archive attributes set, without modifying the attribute (**see** ATTRIB for more info).
/m	Copies source files that have their archive attributes set and then turns off the archive attribute in the *source* files (**see** ATTRIB for more info).
/d:*date*	Copies source files that have been modified on or after the date specified by the *date* parameter (*mm-dd-yy* is the default format).
/p	Prompts you before creating each destination file.
/s	Copies files in directories and subdirectories unless they are empty.
/e	Copies subdirectories even if they are empty.

(continued)

Variable or Option	Function
/v	Verifies each file as it is written.
/w	Prompts you to press a key before starting the copying process (giving you time to switch disks).
/-y	Forces XCOPY to prompt you before overwriting an existing file.
/y	Allows XCOPY to overwrite existing files without prompting.

Sample

Al in Finance needs a copy of all the files in your \MYTURF directory, including those in the \STUFF and \NONSENSE subdirectories that have been created or modified since February 15, 1998. To make these copies, you enter

```
xcopy c:\myturf\*.* a: /s /d:02/15/95
```

Part IV

Batch Commands

You can create or edit batch files with the DOS Editor if you're running Version 5 or later (*see* "EDIT" in Part III). Pray that you have DOS 5+. If you're using an earlier version of DOS and you're desperate, you can use EDLIN, the terrible DOS line editor.

When editing a batch file, you enter each DOS command on its own line of the file. Type the commands in the order in which you want them played back. If you use a word processor, remember that you have to save your batch file with a BAT extension in a text file format. (Don't save a batch file in the word processor's regular format, or it won't run.)

When creating a batch file, you can use any DOS command that you would normally type at the command prompt. In addition, you can include the special batch file commands included in this section, as appropriate.

The full topic of "Batch File Programming" is best left to books specific to that subject. For now, you may want to have your DOS guru show you a few tricks, or you may just stare slack-jawed in awe of this potentially fun aspect of DOS.

In this part . . .

- ✓ **Controlling what appears on-screen**
- ✓ **Running batch programs**
- ✓ **Creating prompts**

@

Suppresses the display of a command on-screen when DOS executes it.

DOSspeak

@command

where *command* is the DOS command that you don't want displayed.

CALL

Calls one batch program from another without causing the first one to stop. When DOS finishes executing all the commands in the second batch program, it returns to the first program. Then DOS executes the first command under the CALL command that was just executed.

DOSspeak

CALL [*drive:*][*path*]*filename* [*batch-parameters*]

Variable or Option	Function
[*drive:*][*path*]*filename*	Specifies the drive, directory, and name of the batch file you're calling. This *filename* parameter must have a BAT extension.
batch-parameters	Specifies any arguments required by a batch file that contains replaceable parameters.

CHOICE

Prompts you to make a choice in a batch program. You can then branch the batch program depending upon what choice you make (available in DOS 6+ only).

DOSspeak

CHOICE [/c[:]*keys*] [/n] [/s] [/t[:]*c,nn*] [*text*]

Variable or Option	Function
/c[:]*keys*	Specifies which keys are presented as choices in the prompt. When the CHOICE command is executed, the specified keys appear in brackets, separated by commas and terminated with a question mark — for example, [A,B,C]? when you enter /c:abc. If you omit the /c switch, DOS displays [Y,N]? as the default choice.
/n	Suppresses the CHOICE prompt and displays only the message that precedes this prompt (specified by the *text* parameter).
/s	Makes the CHOICE command case sensitive. When the /s switch is not used, both lowercase and uppercase letters are accepted as matches to the *keys* parameters.
/t[:]*c,nn*	Specifies a default key and how long CHOICE is to wait before defaulting to that key. The *c* parameter specifies the default key (it must, however, be one of those specified with the /c switch). The *nn* parameter specifies the number of seconds to pause (between 0 and 99).
text	Specifies the message that you want displayed in front of the CHOICE prompt created with the /c switch. You only need to enclose this text in quotation marks when the text contains the / (forward slash) character. If you omit the *text* parameter, CHOICE displays only the prompt specified with the /c switch.

Sample

To prompt the user to choose between terminating the batch file or continuing, you enter

```
choice /c:qc Quit now, or Continue processing?
```

When you run the batch file with this CHOICE command, on-screen you see

```
Quit now, or Continue processing? [Q,C]?
```

ECHO

Controls whether DOS displays commands in a batch file as it executes them. You can also use ECHO to display your own messages to the user.

DOSspeak

ECHO [on | off]

or

ECHO [*message*]

Variable or Option	Function
on	Turns on ECHO so that DOS commands are displayed as executed (the default setting).
off	Turns off ECHO so that DOS commands are not displayed as executed.
message	Specifies the message you want the user to see even when ECHO is turned off. To insert a blank line in the display with ECHO, type a period with no space after ECHO.

If you enter ECHO without any parameters, DOS tells you whether ECHO is currently on or off.

FOR

Runs a specified DOS command for each file in a set of files.

DOSspeak

FOR %%*variable* in (*set*) do *command* [*command-parameters*]

Variable or Option	Function
%%*variable*	Specifies the name of the variable that you want DOS to assign each item, in turn, in the *set* parameter. When specifying the variable, don't use numbers between 0 and 9, because DOS will confuse these numbers with command line replaceable parameters.
set	Specifies the files, replaceable parameters representing filenames, or text strings that are assigned in sequence to the %%*variable* and then processed by the specified *command*. Files or strings in a set must be separated by a space, and all the items in the entire set must be enclosed in parentheses. When specifying items in the set, you can use wildcard characters.
command	Specifies the DOS command that you want executed (which can be any command other than the FOR command).

Variable or Option	Function
%%variable	Specifies the name of the variable that you want.
command-parameters	Specifies any parameters or switches used by the specified command, including the FOR command's *%%variable* and command line replaceable parameters (%0 through %9).

Sample

To have your batch command delete all files with JNK and BAK extensions in your \MYTURF directory, you enter

```
for %%ext in (\myturf\*.jnk \myturf\*.bak) do del
    %%ext
```

GOTO

Redirects execution in the batch file to a line identified with a particular label.

DOSspeak

```
GOTO label
```

where *label* is the name of the line in the batch file at which execution is to resume. When you label the line in the batch file, the label name must appear alone preceded by a colon.

Sample

To identify the commands on the last two lines of the batch file with the label End, you enter

```
:End
```

on its own line right above the lines with the last two commands. Then, at the place in the batch file where you want execution to jump to these last two commands, you enter

```
goto End
```

IF

Performs conditional processing in the batch program. If the condition in the IF command is true, DOS carries out the specified command. Otherwise, DOS ignores the command.

DOSspeak

```
IF [not] errorlevel number command
```

or

```
IF [not] string1==string2 command
```

or

```
IF [not] exist filename command
```

Variable or Option	Function
not	Specifies that DOS should carry out the specified command only when the condition is not true (that is, when the condition is false).
errorlevel *number*	Specifies a true condition when the previous program executed by COMMAND.COM returned an exit code equal to or greater than the value specified by the *number* parameter.
command	Specifies the DOS command to carry out when the condition is true.
string1==string2	Specifies a true condition when *string1* and *string2* are the same (including case). These *string1* and *string2* parameters can be replaceable parameters (such as %0) or literal strings (such as bigdoc.txt). Literal strings do not have to be enclosed in quotation marks.
exist *filename*	Specifies a true condition when DOS locates the file specified by the *filename* parameter.

Sample

To tell the batch file to jump to the section at the bottom of the file labeled End and execute the commands it finds there if DOS can't locate your BIGDOC.TXT file in your \MYTURF directory, you enter

```
if not exist c:\myturf\bigdoc.txt goto End
```

To display an error message on-screen when this file is not found, you enter instead

```
if not exist c:\myturf\bigdoc.txt echo This file's
   no longer in \MYTURF!
```

PAUSE

Pauses the execution of the batch file until the user presses a key. Optionally, displays your message on-screen while the batch file is paused.

DOSspeak

PAUSE [*message*]

where *message* is the text of the message you want displayed while the program is paused. Note that the user sees the message only when ECHO is on. Whether you enter PAUSE alone or with a *message* parameter, DOS always displays its own user message Press any key to continue during the pause (even when ECHO is off).

REM

Lets you add comments to your batch file that will be displayed when ECHO is on (the default).

If you don't want your comments displayed, precede the REM command with the @ command or, better yet, turn ECHO off with @echo off at the top of the batch file.

DOSspeak

REM [*string*]

where *string* is the text of the comments that you want to add to the batch file.

SHIFT

Modifies the position of the replaceable parameters in a batch program by discarding the %0 parameter and then moving each subsequent parameter to a lower number (%1 to %0, %2 to %1, and so on).

The SHIFT command lets you specify more than ten replaceable parameters (%0 to %9) in the command line. Use SHIFT as often as you need it to process all the command arguments. Just keep in mind that each time you use SHIFT, DOS discards the %0 replace-able parameter.

DOSspeak

SHIFT

Part V

Configuration Commands

Configuration commands go in a special file: CONFIG.SYS (pronounced *config-dot-sis*). Because the CONFIG.SYS file, like the AUTOEXEC.BAT file, is used each time you start the computer, you need to make sure that this file is located in the root directory of the drive from which your computer boots, meaning drive C.

Like the AUTOEXEC.BAT file, the CONFIG.SYS file is a text file containing a list of commands that DOS is to execute when you boot the computer. Because it consists of text, you can edit this file with any word processor that deals with text files, the DOS Editor (the EDIT command in Version 5), or EDLIN. Ugh, EDLIN.

When editing your CONFIG.SYS file, you can include any of the configuration commands covered in this section.

In this part . . .

- ✔ **Checking for premature program termination**
- ✔ **Customizing and optimizing memory use**
- ✔ **Using foreign conventions**
- ✔ **Loading and defining devices**
- ✔ **Customizing startup menus**
- ✔ **Making file and disk specifications**
- ✔ **Loading memory-resident (terminate-and-stay-resident) programs**
- ✔ **. . . And more!**

BREAK

Tells DOS how often to check for the Ctrl+C or Ctrl+Break keys used to terminate a program or batch file prematurely.

This command is safe only in the hands of a programmer or some other totally DOSsed person. Stay clear unless they give you hazard pay.

DOSspeak

```
BREAK=[on | off]
```

Variable or Option	Function
on	Turns on extended Ctrl+C checking so that DOS checks during read and write operations as well as when it reads from the keyboard or writes to the screen or a printer.
off	Turns off extended Ctrl+C checking.

BUFFERS

Allocates memory for a number of disk buffers when you start your computer.

In versions prior to 3.3, DOS uses 2 as the default number of buffers. In Versions 3.3+, the number depends on how your system is configured (with 15 being the default on a computer with 512K or more RAM).

DOSspeak

```
BUFFERS=n[,m]
```

Variable or Option	Function
n	Specifies the number of disk buffers (between 1 and 99).
m	Specifies the number of buffers in the secondary buffer cache (between 1 and 8).

COUNTRY

Configures DOS to recognize the character set, the sort order, and the punctuation, date, time, and currency conventions for a particular country.

DOSspeak

COUNTRY=*xxx*[.[*yyy*][.[*drive:*][*path*]*filename*]]

Variable or Option	Function
xxx	Specifies the COUNTRY code. The *xxx* parameter is a three-digit number, corresponding to the international dialing prefix of the country, including any leading zeros necessary to make up three digits.
yyy	Specifies the code page, which in turn specifies the character set to use (*see* the table in the KEYB entry in Part III).
[*drive:*][*path*]*filename*	Specifies the drive, directory, and name of the file containing the country information. If you omit the *drive:* and *path* parameters, DOS assumes that the file is in the search directory (*see* PATH in Part III). If you omit the *filename* parameter as well, DOS uses the COUNTRY.SYS file.

Sample

To enable Cousin Olaf to use the Norwegian keyboard, sort order, dates and times, and the whole Nordic ten yards on your computer, you add

```
country=047,865
```

to your CONFIG.SYS file.

DEVICE

Loads a particular device driver into memory so that your computer can use that device.

When you have multiple devices to specify, you enter multiple DEVICE commands in your CONFIG.SYS file. Be aware, however, that the order in which these devices are loaded can be critical — so check your documentation for details. The standard device drivers in DOS 6 include ANSI.SYS, DISPLAY.SYS, DRIVER.SYS, DBLSPACE.SYS, EGA.SYS, EMM386.EXE, HIMEM.SYS, INTERLNK.EXE, POWER.EXE, RAMDRIVE.SYS, SETVER.EXE, and SMARTDRV.SYS. For specific information on any of these device drivers, at the DOS prompt, type help followed by the device driver filename, for example

```
help interlnk.exe
```

DOSspeak

```
DEVICE=[drive:][path]filename [dd-parameters]
```

Variable or Option	Function
[drive:][path]filename	Specifies the drive, directory, and name of the device driver file. If you omit the drive: and path parameters, DOS assumes that the driver file is on the disk and directory used to boot the computer.
dd-parameters	Specifies any command line information required by the device driver.

DEVICEHIGH

Loads a particular device driver into the upper memory of your 386, 486, or Pentium computer, freeing more conventional memory for your application programs.

This command is safe only in the hands of a programmer or some other totally DOSsed person. Stay clear unless they give you hazard pay.

DOSspeak

```
DEVICEHIGH=[drive:][path]filename [dd-parameters]
```

or

```
DEVICEHIGH=[/l:region1[,minsize1][;region2[minsize2]
    [/s]]=[drive:][path]filename [dd-parameters]
```

Variable or Option	Function
[drive:][path]filename	Specifies the drive, directory, and name of the device driver file that you want to load into upper memory. If you omit the drive: and path parameters, DOS assumes that the driver file is on the disk and directory used to boot the computer. By default, DOS loads the driver into the largest free upper memory block (UMB) and makes all other UMBs available for the driver's use.
dd-parameters	Specifies any command line information required by the device driver.
(/l:region1[,minsize1] [;region2[,minsize]])	Specifies one or more regions of memory in which the device driver is to be loaded. To ensure that a driver won't be loaded into a region that's too small for it, you can also specify the minsize parameter for the particular region parameter that you specify.

Variable or Option	Function
/s	Normally used by the MemMaker program to shrink the UMB (upper memory block) to its minimum size while the device drive is loading. Don't use this /s switch unless you're certain that shrinking the UMB won't interfere with loading the device driver. You can only use the /s switch with the /l switch and when you've specified both a *region* and a *minsize* parameter.

To find out how a particular device driver uses memory, enter the MEM command with the /m switch and the device driver's filename. Also, your CONFIG.SYS file must contain the following commands to make the upper memory area available for loading device drivers before you use the DEVICEHIGH command:

```
device=c:\dos\himem.sys
device=c:\dos\emm386.exe ram
dos=umb
```

DOS

Enables DOS to load part of itself into the High Memory Area (HMA) and/or maintain a link with the upper memory blocks (UMBs) of reserved memory (available with Versions 5+).

You must load the device driver HIMEM.SYS or some other extended memory manager before you configure DOS to UMB or HIGH. Unless you're being watched over by a programmer or some other DOSsed person, avoid using this command.

DOSspeak

```
DOS=high | low[,umb |,noumb]
```

or

```
DOS=[high, | low,]umb | noumb
```

Variable or Option	Function
high	Causes DOS to load part of itself into the HMA.
low	Causes DOS to load itself into conventional memory (the default).
umb	Causes DOS to establish a link to the UMBs in reserved memory that can be used by the LOADHIGH DOS command or DEVICEHIGH configuration command.
noumb	Causes DOS not to establish a link with reserved memory.

DRIVPARM

Defines parameters for devices such as disk and tape drives when you start your computer.

You can include multiple DRIVPARM commands in your CONFIG.SYS, each one defining the characteristics of a particular floppy or tape drive in your system.

This command is safe only in the hands of a programmer or some other totally DOSsed person. Stay clear unless they give you hazard pay.

DOSspeak

```
DRIVPARM=/d:number [/c] [/f:factor] [/h:heads] [/i]
    [/n] [/s:sectors] [t:tracks]
```

Variable or Option	Function
/d:*number*	Specifies the number of a physical drive between 0 and 255, where 0 = drive A, 1 = drive B, 2 = drive C, and so on.
/c	Specifies that the drive can detect when the door is closed.
/f:*factor*	Specifies the drive type. The factor parameter can be any of the following: 0 (for 160/180K or 320/360K, 5¹/₄-inch), 1 (for 1.2MB, 5¹/₄-inch), 2 (for 720K, 3¹/₂-inch), 5 (for a hard disk), 6 (for a tape backup), 7 (for 1.44MB, 3¹/₂-inch), 8 (for a read/write optical disk), or 9 (for 2.88MB, 3¹/₂-inch).
/h:*heads*	Specifies the maximum number of heads (1 through 99).
/i	(Versions 4+) Specifies that the drive is an electronically compatible 3¹/₂-inch floppy drive (that is, one that uses your existing floppy-disk-drive controller).
/n	Specifies that the drive is nonremovable.
/s:*sectors*	Specifies the number of sectors per track (1 through 99).
/t:*tracks*	Specifies the number of tracks per side (1 through 999).

FCBS (File Control Blocks)

Specifies the number of file control blocks (FCBs) that DOS can open at one time (in case you care, FCBs are data structures that reside in an application's memory area and maintain pointers to open files).

Don't fool around with the FCBS configuration command unless your application program puts a gun to your head and forces you to change the number of file control blocks. Most of the new programs use file handles (*see* FILES) instead of FCBs, so you can relax.

DOSspeak

FCBS=*x*[,*y*]

Variable or Option	Function
x	Specifies the maximum number between 1 and 255 (4 is the default) of file control blocks that DOS can have open at one time.
y	(Versions 4+) Specifies the number between 0 and 225 inclusive (the default is 0) of file control blocks that are protected from automatic closure. The *y* parameter must always be less than or equal to the *x* parameter.

FILES

Specifies the number of files that can be open at one time.

DOSspeak

FILES=*x*

where *x* specifies the maximum number between 8 and 255 (the default is 8) of files that can be open at one time.

Sample

Many of the more modern application programs require at least 20 files to be open at one time. To increase the files open to this number in your CONFIG.SYS file, you enter

files=20

INCLUDE

Includes the contents of one menu item within another on a startup menu that lets the user choose between multiple configurations in a single CONFIG.SYS file (available in DOS 6+ only).

For more information on defining multiple configurations in a single CONFIG.SYS file, *see* MENUCOLOR, MENUDEFAULT, MENUITEM, and SUBMENU in this part.

This command is safe only in the hands of a programmer or some other totally DOSsed person. Stay clear unless they give you hazard pay.

DOSspeak

```
INCLUDE=blockname
```

where *blockname* specifies the name of the menu item (also known as a *configuration block*) whose commands you want to include in another menu item.

Sample

Suppose that you've created a startup menu that gives the user a choice between a basic configuration (called basic_config) and a standard configuration (called norm_config) when starting the computer. When defining the standard configuration menu item, you can include the commands already defined for the basic menu item by entering an INCLUDE command, such as the following, after the standard configuration block header (the name of the block enclosed in brackets):

```
[norm_config]
include=basic_config
```

Then, following this INCLUDE command, you place the rest of the configuration commands beyond those in the basic configuration that are unique to the standard configuration.

INSTALL

Loads a memory-resident program into memory when you start your computer. These programs are also known as terminate-and-stay-resident (TSR) programs.

Place all INSTALL commands after the DEVICE commands in your CONFIG.SYS file because you can't load a memory-resident program before a device driver. Also, don't use INSTALL to load memory-resident programs that use environment variables, shortcut keys, or require COMMAND.COM to be present to handle errors.

DOSspeak

```
INSTALL=[drive:][path]filename [command-parameters]
```

Variable or Option	Function
[*drive:*][*path*]*filename*	Specifies the drive, directory, and name of the memory-resident program to load. These programs routinely include FASTOPEN.EXE, KEYB.COM, NLSFUNC.EXE, and SHARE.EXE. If you omit the *drive:* and *path* parameters, DOS assumes that the file is in the search path (**see** PATH in Part III).
command-parameters	Specifies the parameters for the memory-resident program you are running.

Sample

To have DOS load the Norwegian keyboard program into memory for Cousin Olaf when he starts the computer, you enter

```
install=keyb.com no,865
```

in the CONFIG.SYS file.

LASTDRIVE

Specifies the maximum number of drives that DOS recognizes.

DOSspeak

```
LASTDRIVE=x
```

where *x* is the letter of the last drive on your computer (A through Z). If you do not include a LASTDRIVE command in your CONFIG.SYS file, the last valid drive on your computer is the letter following the last drive in use. (So if the computer has A, B, C, the default last drive is D.)

MENUCOLOR

Sets the text and background colors for the startup menu that lets the user choose between multiple configurations in a single CONFIG.SYS file (available in DOS 6 only).

For more information on defining multiple configurations in a single CONFIG.SYS file, **see** INCLUDE, MENUDEFAULT, MENUITEM, and SUBMENU in this part.

DOSspeak

```
MENUCOLOR=x[,y]
```

Variable or Option	Function
x	Specifies the color of the menu text (between 0 and 15 — see the table that follows).
y	Specifies the color of the background screen (between 0 and 15 — see the table that follows). If you omit the y parameter, DOS uses black for the background.

Your *x* and *y* parameters can be any of the parameters in the following table. When choosing *x* and *y* parameters, however, be sure that you select contrasting colors, or you won't be able to read your menu!

Value	Color	Value	Color
0	Black	8	Gray
1	Blue	9	Bright blue
2	Green	10	Bright green
3	Cyan	11	Bright cyan
4	Red	12	Bright red
5	Magenta	13	Bright magenta
6	Brown	14	Yellow
7	White	15	Bright white

MENUDEFAULT

Specifies the default menu item for a startup menu that lets the user choose between multiple configurations in a single CONFIG.SYS file (available in DOS 6+ only).

For more information on defining multiple configurations in a single CONFIG.SYS file, *see* INCLUDE, MENUCOLOR, MENUITEM, and SUBMENU in this part.

DOSspeak

MENUDEFAULT=*blockname*[,*timeout*]

Variable or Option	Function
blockname	Specifies the name of the menu item that you want the startup menu to default to.

Variable or Option	Function
timeout	Specifies the number of seconds (between 0 and 90) that DOS waits before starting the computer with the default menu item specified by the *blockname* parameter. If you omit the *timeout* parameter, DOS uses a timeout of 0 seconds, which gives the user no chance ever to choose any of the other menu items — not too bright to give 'em options and then not allow them to choose.

Sample

Suppose that you've created a startup menu that gives the user a choice between using a basic configuration (called `basic_config`) and a standard configuration (called `norm_config`) when starting the computer. To make the standard configuration the default that DOS automatically uses if the user doesn't choose the basic one within 20 seconds, you enter

```
menudefault=norm_config,20
```

as the last command in the configuration block identified as [menu] that defines which menu items appear on the main menu (*see* MENUITEM for details).

MENUITEM

Specifies the menu items to be included in a startup menu that lets the user choose between multiple configurations in a single CONFIG.SYS file (available in DOS 6+ only).

For more information on defining multiple configurations in a single CONFIG.SYS file, *see* INCLUDE, MENUCOLOR, MENUDEFAULT, and SUBMENU in this part.

DOSspeak

```
MENUITEM=blockname[,menu_text]
```

Variable or Option	Function
blockname	Specifies the name of the menu or submenu item that identifies what configuration commands are to be carried out when the user selects the menu item. If the MENUITEM command defines a main menu item, it must be located in the configuration block identified with the [menu] heading. If the MENUITEM command defines a submenu item, it must be located in the configuration block identified by the blockname used in the SUBMENU command.

(continued)

Variable or Option	Function
	The configuration block containing the commands carried out when the user selects the menu item must then be defined elsewhere in the CONFIG.SYS file and identified with the *blockname* specified in the MENUITEM command enclosed in brackets. When the user chooses the menu item, DOS carries out all commands in this configuration block as well as all commands in a configuration block identified by the [common] heading.
menu_text	Specifies the text you want DOS to display after the menu number it assigns to the menu item (up to 70 characters).

Sample

To create a menu with two menu items that lets the user choose between a basic and a standard configuration, you enter

```
[menu]
menuitem=basic_config,Basic Configuration
menuitem=norm_config,Good Old Standard
    Configuration
```

Then, when you start your computer, DOS displays the following startup menu:

```
MS-DOS 6 Startup Menu
=====================
1. Basic Configuration
2. Good Old Standard Configuration
```

NUMLOCK

Specifies whether the Num Lock key is set to on or off when you start your computer (available in DOS 6+ only).

NUMLOCK is one of the six new commands for defining startup menus and multiple configurations for your system. ***See also*** INCLUDE, MENUCOLOR, MENUITEM, and SUBMENU.

This command can confuse a user who expects the keys to do one thing and finds that they're doing something else. If you're not sure of what you're doing, leave this command alone.

DOSspeak

```
NUMLOCK=[on | off]
```

Variable or Option	Function
on	Turns on the Num Lock key when DOS displays the startup menu.
off	Turns off the Num Lock key when DOS displays the startup menu.

SHELL

Specifies the name and location of the command interpreter (COMMAND.COM unless you specify another).

You don't need to add a SHELL command to your CONFIG.SYS file unless you've put the COMMAND.COM in some directory besides the root directory of the disk you boot from (drive C in almost all cases), or unless you want to use some other shell (that is, interface) you've cooked up or come across in your travels.

DOSspeak

SHELL=[[*drive:*]*path*]*filename* [parameters]

Variable or Option	Function
[[*drive:*]*path*]*filename*	Specifies the drive, directory, and name of the file containing the command interpreter. If you omit the *drive:* and *path* parameters, DOS looks in the root directory of the disk you boot from.
parameters	Specifies any command line parameters or switches that can be used with the command interpreter specified by the *filename* parameter.

STACKS

Specifies the number and size of the data stacks used to handle hardware interrupts.

The default settings for the STACKS commands are 0,0 for the IBM PC, IBM PC/XT, and IBM PC-Portable computers and 9,128 for all other computers.

Don't fool around with the STACKS command unless you're getting those wonderful Stack Overflow error messages before your computer bombs, or your application program demands you to, or the devil makes you do it.

DOSspeak

STACKS=*n*,*s*

Variable or Option	Function
n	Specifies the number of stacks (0 or numbers between 8 and 64).
s	Specifies the size (in bytes) of each stack (0 or numbers between 32 and 512).

SUBMENU

Specifies a submenu item on a startup menu that, when chosen, displays a menu of further choices to the user. Startup menus are used to let the user choose between multiple configurations in a single CONFIG.SYS file (available in DOS 6+ only).

For more information on defining multiple configurations in a single CONFIG.SYS file, **see** INCLUDE, MENUCOLOR, MENUDEFAULT, and MENUITEM in this part.

DOSspeak

SUBMENU=*blockname*[,*menu_text*]

Variable or Option	Function
blockname	Specifies the name of the submenu containing the menu items that are to be displayed when the user chooses the submenu item. The SUBMENU command must be located in the configuration block identified with the [menu] heading. The MENUITEM commands specifying the new menu items — to be displayed when the user selects the submenu item on the main menu — are placed in a separate configuration block identified with the *blockname* parameter specified in the SUBMENU command enclosed in brackets.
menu_text	Specifies the text you want DOS to display after the menu number that it assigns to the submenu item (up to 70 characters).

Sample

Suppose that instead of defaulting to the standard configuration, when a user chooses the standard rather than the basic on the main menu, you want to offer a further choice: a submenu between an enhanced and the plain-vanilla standard configuration.

To do so, you enter

```
[menu]
menuitem=basic_config,Basic Configuration
submenu=standmenu,Standard Configuration
[standmenu]
menuitem=enhanc_config,Souped-Up Standard
     Configuration
menuitem=norm_config, Plain Old Standard
     Configuration
```

Then, when you start the computer, DOS displays the following startup menu on your screen:

```
MS-DOS 6 Startup Menu
=====================
1. Basic Configuration
2. Standard Configuration
```

If the user chooses option 2. Standard Configuration, DOS replaces the main menu with the following submenu of choices:

```
MS-DOS 6 Startup Menu
=====================
1. Souped-Up Standard Configuration
2. Plain Old Standard Configuration
```

SWITCHES

Does a number of wacky things, such as specifying that an enhanced keyboard work like an older keyboard, telling DOS that the WINA20.386 file has been moved out of the root directory, preventing you from using the F5 or F8 key to bypass the startup command, or skipping the two-second delay after displaying the DOS startup message.

This command is safe only in the hands of a programmer or some other totally DOSsed person. Stay clear unless they give you hazard pay.

DOSspeak

```
SWITCHES=[/k] [/w] [/n] [/f]
```

Variable or Option	Function
/k	Forces an enhanced (101-key) keyboard to act like an older (84-key) keyboard. This switch is used only when running an older program that can't deal with the enhanced keyboard arrangement.

(continued)

Variable or Option	Function
/w	Tells DOS that the WINA20.386 file has been moved to a directory other than the root directory so that you can run Windows 3.0 on a 386 computer. When you use this switch, your CONFIG.SYS file must also contain a DEVICE command indicating the correct whereabouts of the WINA20.386.
/n	Prevents you from using the F5 or F8 key to bypass startup commands (not that you would anyway).
/f	Skips the two-second delay after displaying the `Starting MS-DOS. . .` message when you boot the computer.

When using the SWITCHES command in your CONFIG.SYS file, you can combine the various switches in one file by separating each switch with a space as follows:

```
switches=/k /n /f
```

Techie Talk

See also *DOS For Dummies,* Windows 98 Edition.

ASCII file: Plain text file that you can view by using the TYPE command. These files contain regular alphabetical-numerical characters, not computer code, in the ASCII (American Standard Code for Information Interchange) format.

attributes: Characteristics of a file that determine whether you can modify, delete, and/or view the file. Files can be marked as read-only, with an archive flag, as a system file, or as a hidden file.

bad sectors: Defective, unusable portions of a disk. If the CHKDSK command reveals that your floppy disk has bad sectors, use another disk instead. If your hard disk has bad sectors, use a hard-disk diagnostic program.

batch file or program: A collection of DOS commands saved in a text file with the BAT extension. When you type the filename at the DOS prompt, DOS executes each command in the batch file — as if you had typed the commands in manually. The most famous batch file in DOS is the AUTOEXEC.BAT file.

binary file: A file containing only computer code (bits and bytes), no regular text.

buffer: A temporary storage area in memory, used especially when slower components need to catch up.

cache: A temporary storage area in memory for frequently accessed code or data.

command interpreter: The part of DOS that displays prompts, interprets commands and batch files, and loads and executes application programs.

command line: Text you type after the DOS prompt.

command prompt: See **DOS prompt.**

compression: Process that maximizes the drive space available.

configuration commands: Commands to tell DOS how your system is put together so that the application programs you run can take advantage of the particular memory arrangement or hardware devices attached to your computer — unlike standard DOS commands that you enter at the DOS command line or put into a batch file, which tell DOS to do something specific, such as delete a file or format a disk. Also unlike those standard commands, configuration commands are always placed in a special file — CONFIG.SYS (pronounced *config-dot-sis*) — that is read into your computer's memory the first thing each time you start your PC.

defragmenting: Reorganizing the files on a disk so that all parts of each file are written to contiguous (adjacent) sectors. Optimizes disk performance.

directory: Grouping of files in a single location. A directory can be further divided into subdirectories. Use the DIR command to view the contents of a directory.

DOS prompt: The letter of the current drive followed by > that you see on-screen when DOS is ready to receive a command (you can customize the prompt by using the PROMPT command). You type the command right after the DOS prompt.

density, disk: Refers to how much information the disk can store. A double-density 3$\frac{1}{2}$-inch disk can hold up to 720K of data; a high-density 3$\frac{1}{2}$-inch disk can hold up to 1.44MB of data.

drive, disk: Physical device where you store files. A drive can be a floppy disk drive, a hard disk drive, a CD-ROM drive, or a network drive.

extension: The optional letters that appear after the period in a filename. An extension consists of one to three characters and usually indicates in which program the file was created.

FAT32: A new version of the File Allocation Table file system that lets you format disks over 2GB as a single drive.

file: Collection of information stored on a disk or disc (a floppy disk, a CD-ROM, the hard disk drive).

formatting a disk: Process of preparing a disk so that DOS can store files on it. If the disk isn't empty, formatting it wipes out the old files.

fragmented: See **defragmenting.**

hidden file: A file whose attributes are set so that it doesn't show up in a directory listing. Such files are usually hidden for a good reason — so that users don't accidentally modify or delete important information.

hot key: The highlighted letter in a menu or command name on-screen that allows you to access that file or command by pressing the Alt key and the letter simultaneously. In DOS, hot keys appear in bold; in Windows, hot keys are underlined.

lost clusters in chains: Another name for bits of fragmented files. See **defragmenting.**

macro: A program within a program that automates tasks or procedures. Batch files are a type of macro used in DOS.

memory, conventional versus upper: *Conventional* memory, the first 640K of a PC's random-access memory (RAM), is what DOS uses for running programs; *upper* memory is the rest of the memory, which you can make use of with certain commands, such as MEMMAKER in DOS 6.

memory-resident program: See **terminate-and-stay-resident (TSR) program.**

multitasking: Running one program in the background while you work in another program. In Windows 95, you can multitask a DOS program by clicking the Background button on the DOS toolbar.

operating system: Software that controls your computer. DOS, UNIX, and System 7.*x* for the Macintosh are popular operating systems.

output: What you get after you input commands. Can be characters on-screen, a printout, or sound from the speakers.

parameter: Option or argument that you add to commands to modify the result.

path or pathname: The location of a file, indicated by the drive letter followed by a colon and the hierarchy of directories, separated by slashes. From left to right, the pathname goes from general (the drive) to specific (the actual filename or desired directory name).

pipe character: The vertical bar — | — that appears in commands and sends the result of one DOS command to another. Also, a DOSspeak convention that indicates when you have a choice of parameters to enter.

port, parallel and serial: *Ports* are the connections on the PC where you attach external items. The *parallel* port is usually where you plug in the printer; the *serial* port is where you plug in a modem, mouse, printer, scanner, or a number of other peripherals.

RAM (random-access memory): The computer's primary memory, where programs and data are stored for quick access. When you turn off the computer or exit a program, the RAM contents are lost.

read-only: File attribute that prevents the user from modifying the file's contents. You can read the file's data, but you can't write to the file.

reboot: To restart the computer, either by shutting it off and then turning it on again (a *cold* boot) or pressing a reset button or Ctrl+Alt+Delete (a *warm* boot). Never reboot your computer unless a program tells you to or the computer stops responding to your commands.

root directory: The first directory on a disk, from which all other directories branch out.

Registry: A collection of files that hold configuration information for you computer.

secondary mouse button: The nonprimary button on the mouse. Unless you've adjusted your mouse's settings so that the primary button is the right button (which you may want to do if you're left handed), your secondary mouse button is the one on the right. Clicking the secondary mouse button is often referred to as *right-clicking* (in this right-hand–dominated society).

sectors: Divisions of a *track* on a disk. See **track.**

shell: A menu-driven utility that enables you to perform many basic DOS tasks without having to type DOS commands.

Shortcut: A picture you can click on to open a program or data file.

Start menu: The menu that pops up when you click the Start button on the Windows 95 taskbar. From this menu, you can access programs and documents and open a DOS window.

switch: A command option or parameter, starting with a slash or a dash, following the command that it affects.

system file: A file containing information that the computer needs. Don't mess with system files (like those ending in .SYS, .COM, or .DRV).

taskbar: The row of pictures (usually at the bottom of the screen) in Windows 95 that indicates what programs are currently open. The Start button is at the beginning of the taskbar.

terminate-and-stay-resident (TSR) program: Also known as a *memory-resident program.* A type of program that always stays in RAM and is activated by a keystroke, even while another program is also in memory.

toolbar: The row of buttons (usually at the top of the screen) that gives you quick access to certain commands. In Windows 95, the DOS screen features a toolbar that lets you run DOS in the background, change the screen font, and more.

track: The defining area of data storage on a disk. A disk is divided into *tracks,* which are further divided into *sectors.*

URL: Uniform Resource Locator. An address for a document on the World Wide Web.

utility: Program that fixes or enhances your system. Unlike an application, a utility does not produce real output.

variable: A symbol that represents a value or text in a program. That value can change during the course of the program.

volume: A disk (floppy or hard). A *volume label* is the name that you can assign the disk.

wildcard: A character or symbol that can stand for any character or group of characters in a filename when performing a search.

Index

D

(continued)

E

Y

Notes

_____
_____
_____
_____
_____
_____
_____
_____
_____
_____
_____
_____
_____
_____
_____
_____
_____
_____
_____
_____

Notes

FOR DUMMIES
BOOK REGISTRATION

Register
This Book
and Win!

We want to hear from you!

Visit **dummies.com** to register this book and tell us how you liked it!

- Get entered in our monthly prize giveaway.

- Give us feedback about this book — tell us what you like best, what you like least, or maybe what you'd like to ask the author and us to change!

- Let us know any other *For Dummies* topics that interest you.

Your feedback helps us determine what books to publish, tells us what coverage to add as we revise our books, and lets us know whether we're meeting your needs as a *For Dummies* reader. You're our most valuable resource, and what you have to say is important to us!

Not on the Web yet? It's easy to get started with *Dummies 101: The Internet For Windows 98* or *The Internet For Dummies* at local retailers everywhere.

Or let us know what you think by sending us a letter at the following address:

For Dummies Book Registration
Dummies Press
10475 Crosspoint Blvd.
Indianapolis, IN 46256

™

STSELLING
BOOK SERIES